Kingdom Parables

TWELVE SIGNPOSTS TO GUIDE YOU THROUGH TURBULENT TIMES

PIERRE G. ROSA

PUBLISHERS

To George Cuff:

mentor, role model, and friend.

CONTENTS

ACKNOWLEDGMENTS

Jesus has fascinated me since the first day I heard about Him, thirty years ago. Now He allows me to share this fascination on the printed page. Words cannot describe my gratitude for such unimaginable honor. May I decrease so that my Majestic Savior, who has repeatedly guided me through turbulent times, increase.

Denise and Julia (aka my girls), along with my dear mother Nicole and the Griffins, have supported me throughout this project. Aware of the demands of writing, they prayed for me diligently and offered constant encouragement.

My fellow elders at Grace Baptist Church (GBC) granted me the time to study, write, and shepherd while they attended to other needs of our thriving congregation. I am indebted to Brian Schmidt, Jonsey Hendrix, and Bob Mathisen, men of surpassing character and integrity. Their Christlikeness motivates me to pursue excellence.

The people of GBC honor me with attentiveness, thoughtfulness, loyalty, and appreciation. I don't deserve such love, and yet this distinguished flock personifies clearly the virtue that bears the name of our church.

Working with AMG has brought me tremendous joy and growth. Our shared love for the Word, commitment to sound doctrine, and passion for gospel advancement are hallmarks of our partnership. Notably, Amanda Jenkins provided valuable insight and wise feedback for the completion of a final product worthy to be placed alongside so many excellent titles.

About the Author

Pierre Rosa was born and raised in Brazil. After coming to faith in Christ, he moved to the United States in 1997 to further his education and study for ministry. For ten years, he served as an associate pastor at Shadow Mountain Community Church in San Diego, California, under his role model, Dr. David Jeremiah. Pierre is now the senior pastor of Grace Baptist Church in Salem, Oregon.

After moving north, he and his friend Brian Schmidt started *Truth with Grace*, a ministry dedicated to broadcasting Pierre's sermons around the world. *TwG* is featured in eleven radio stations in the Pacific Northwest and the Midwest as well as other media platforms, such as sermonaudio.com.

Pierre graduated from San Diego Christian College (BA, biblical studies) and Southern California Seminary (MDiv), where he also taught classes on evangelism and missions. In 2014 he received his doctor of ministry degree from Southwestern Baptist Theological Seminary with a focus on expository preaching.

When he is not exploring the Pacific Northwest with his wife, Denise, and daughter, Julia (and sometimes their springer spaniel, Bono), Pierre is studying, writing, shepherding, or practicing Brazilian jiujitsu at the local dojo.

Connect with him and learn about his other books at www.truthwithgrace.org.

PREFACE

I launched the Christmas season of 2019 at Grace Baptist Church by inviting the congregation on a journey through the Gospel of Matthew. Having just finished studying the book of Ruth, pastor and flock shared the excitement of discovering the nature and character of our Kinsman Redeemer, now from the pen of a tax collector turned apostle. I started the sermon series by reminding them that God has gifted humanity by preserving a work that, along with the other canonical Gospels, chronicles the words and works of our Majestic Savior.

Matthew writes a selected biographical narrative (driven by theme rather than chronology) of the life and ministry of Christ. The author's many Old Testament quotes indicate that he reaches Jewish Christians from the first century. His extensive use of the expression "kingdom of heaven," while the other Gospel writers use "kingdom of God," mirrors his Jewish audience's reverence for God's name.

But Matthew also writes to you, the modern-day follower of Christ who craves the security that only a sovereign and divine King can assure. Such an assurance does not come from empty promises of a trouble-free life (a guarantee He never made and a life He never modeled). Even though He endured rejection and opposition from His own kin and despite worldwide calamities today, Jesus's redemptive plan remains unchanged. Not only does He conquer death at the end of the story, but He also commissions you to carry on the work of disciple-making. Can you think of anything more dignified and rewarding?

In this book, you and I will discover the features of the good news Jesus commissioned us to proclaim. We will unfold the kingdom parables in Matthew 13 as a road map that leads us to joy in turbulent times. I titled the first part of this volume "His Revered Majesty." Since this book is a part of a character studies series, this section will build a solid foundation by focusing on the identity, beauty, and majesty of our Lord. I recommend reading one chapter a day of this preliminary part in preparation for the twelve weeks of study, which starts in part 2, "The Royal Mysteries." Then, following the chronology of the life of Christ, I will take you to chapter 10 of the first Gospel so that we can understand how our Majestic Savior enlists and equips His people to accomplish His redemptive work. I titled part three "The Regal Mission."

This volume will

- arouse your emotions and stimulate your intellect;

- apply proper exegesis and an inductive approach to Bible study;

- demonstrate the harmony of Scripture, drawing from the broader context of the Bible;

- address the decline of Christianity in Western society; and

- highlight the opportunities for gospel proclamation that adversity brings.

- I pray that after reading this book, you will

- grasp God's redemptive plan for the time between the advent and return of Christ,

- rejoice in your role in God's kingdom program,

- rekindle your desire for heaven,

- be equipped to facilitate home Bible study groups using this material, and

- be emboldened to share the gospel with unsaved family and friends.

Whether you decide to explore these twelve signposts by yourself for personal growth, or in a home study group, I suggest using this resource with an open Bible to search the references as you answer the discussion questions. I also recommend reading the Gospel of Matthew several times through.

Forever your brother,
Pierre Rosa

INTRODUCTION

In January of 2020 a virus that wears a *corona* (Spanish for "crown") crossed borders, devastating economies, destroying livelihoods, shattering travel plans, and killing businesses. This conquering king claimed millions of lives (as of May 2022, the coronavirus caused 6,281,385 casualties worldwide).[1] He imprisoned us in our homes, held us hostage to fear and threatened to divide our churches.

Because we survived epidemics before, we thought that "fifteen days to flatten the curve" would fend off the new despot, but it flattened our hope. We encouraged one another to "stay home; save lives," only to see fellow church members bicker over civil disobedience, with masked believers on one side and unmasked Christians on the other. We sheltered in place, worked remotely, and socially distanced, but the killer monarch dispatched his variants.

When summer 2020 arrived, something else went viral. Cities in America burned to the ground. Throngs rioted, mobs clashed, celebrities tweeted, candidates campaigned, corporations canceled, and we ranted on social media. Meanwhile, pharmaceutical companies raced at warp speed to secure government contracts while health experts predicted a dark winter.

The rest of the world, who mocked our presidential debates, now watched attorneys threaten to release a metaphorical kraken to "stop the steal." Politicians demanded recounts and reopenings while a shirtless shaman, apparently sent by Q, stormed the US Capitol building. Others followed.

When the world expected a return to normalcy, we witnessed the terrorist organization Hamas fire thousands of rockets at Israel. Thankfully, the Iron Dome (Israel's air defense system) prevented carnage in the Holy Land.

What a disastrous way to start a decade! No wonder we littered one another's social media profiles with 2020 and 2021 memes. Since my family and I moved to the United States in the late '90s, I have not experienced a more bizarre season.

---

1. "Coronavirus Resource Center," Johns Hopkins University & Medicine, accessed May 25, 2022, https://coronavirus.jhu.edu.

I suspect you have a similar perspective. Perhaps you wonder if the chaos triggered by COVID-19 and the political unrest of the new decade interrupted the advance of God's redemptive program.

The disciples of Jesus shared a comparable fear. They had just welcomed a legitimate King, but when the religious elite of their time accused Christ of operating by satanic power, the apostles may have assumed their Master failed to honor the offer of the kingdom of heaven, which was at hand.

Jesus could have dispatched more than twelve legions of angels to round up and execute His enemies. Instead, He addressed His audience from a boat, assuring them that God's redemptive plan was on schedule. Not every listener understood His teaching style, but His closest friends received the indescribable blessing of learning the mysteries of the kingdom of heaven followed by the honor of announcing its nearness.

You and I are equally blessed. Join me on a quest for joy amid widespread uncertainty. We will verify that nothing can stop the progress of God's redemptive plan. We will also learn to respond accordingly to anxiety, distress, fear, loss, rejection, and opposition (afflictions present in the world during the absence of the King of kings—the time between his ascension and second coming).

Because any believer who diligently studies Scripture can understand the discourses of Christ, you can use this volume as a resource to encourage anyone who might question Jesus, like John the Baptist did: "Are You the Expected One, or shall we look for someone else?" (Matthew 11:3).

The kingdom of heaven did not take a break at the dawn of this new decade. God still speaks, saves, surprises, sustains, succeeds, satisfies, and secures. Jesus still shepherds, seeks, serves, sanctifies, strengthens, and shocks.

PART ONE
HIS REVERED MAJESTY

A Messianic Ancestry

Compiling genealogical documents would pose no difficulties for tax collectors hired by Rome in the first century AD in Israel. Known as publicans, they had a way with transaction records. The Jews considered them traitors because these agents taxed their own people in exchange for a generous commission from the pagan and oppressive government. Levi (aka Matthew), one such man, worked his trade until the Jewish carpenter everyone talked about invited him: "Follow me" (Matthew 9:9). Without hesitation the tax collector turned Gospel writer immediately left everything behind to answer the call (Luke 5:27–28).

As far as we know, Matthew did not, like his colleague of small stature Zacchaeus, reimburse his countrymen he had defrauded over the years. But he gave the world something much better: "The record of the genealogy of Jesus the Messiah, the son of David, the son of Abraham" (Matthew 1:1). He quotes more Old Testament references than the other three evangelists combined and assumes his readers already know Bible characters such as David and Abraham, because he writes to a Jewish audience. Some of his readers may have been Christians, while others were possibly hostile to Christ.

God's gift to humanity, the four canonical Gospels, reveal selected words and works of Jesus. The first of these biographies in the Bible alternates between sections of discourse and narrative after the prologue. Throughout the book, the author presents the record of the King and chronicles the revelation, rejection, and reception of Christ; explains the resentment of his people toward Jesus; and finally, tells of the resurrection of our Majestic Savior.

Why do I call Jesus the Majestic Savior? Royalty and redemption converge in the person of the long-awaited Messiah, the One to rule the earth physically in the future from Jerusalem.

- Read Matthew 1:1–17 and write what you know about the ancestors of Christ.

We tend to speed-read the genealogies in the Bible because we want to get to what we believe is the meat of the text. But if "all Scripture is inspired by God and profitable for teaching, for reproof, for correction, for training in righteousness" (2 Timothy 3:16), even a list of names from the prologue of the Gospel of Matthew will nourish our souls. The Holy Spirit greets readers of the New Testament with the following three-part, spiritually nutritious genealogical appetizer:

- From the patriarch to the monarch—fourteen generations

- From the monarchy to the captivity (or from Solomon to Babylon)—fourteen generations

- From the deportation to the incarnation—fourteen generations

With that, Matthew demonstrates that no one else other than Jesus can legitimately claim the title of messianic king. Because every descendant of David was a potential Messiah in Jewish thought, any candidate to the throne of Israel would need to prove his ancestry. For this reason, the former tax collector writes in an apologetic tone. (I do not mean he apologizes for what he writes. Rather, the evangelist responds to possible objections concerning the legality of Jesus having the title of *Christos*, the anointed one, translated "Messiah.") Christ is the adopted son of Joseph (1:16), a direct descendant of Judah, the royal tribe of Israel (Genesis 49:10).

Luke the historian traces the Majestic Savior's lineage all the way to Adam, the son of God (Luke 3:38). His Greek audience would have a particular interest in perfect humanity, but he points out that Jesus also belongs to Israel's royal line by blood, through Mary, another descendant of David. He proves, along with Matthew, that by maternal and paternal ancestry Christ is the only One qualified to save humanity from our sins. His genealogy demonstrates His special relationship with redeemed sinners. We start our journey home through turbulent times by identifying four glorious features of this relationship, found in His messianic ancestry.

JESUS WELCOMES MURDERERS

Did you know that David, the first ancestor in this list (and the man after God's own heart), committed murder? It started when he played Peeping Tom in Jerusalem while his armies bled in the battlefield.

- According to 2 Samuel 11:2, what tempted David to pursue this affair? Where was he supposed to be? What does his conduct teach us concerning visually stimulating temptation?

Bathsheba was married. (Matthew purposefully includes the name of her murdered husband in the genealogical record in 1:6, perhaps in memory of Uriah.) Her affair with the king produced an unwanted pregnancy, but after two attempts to hide the scandal, David ordered her husband to the front line of the battle to be killed by enemy arrows.

- Read 2 Samuel 11:6–27, and describe the conspiracy in your own words.

_____

_____

_____

You would think that such dysfunctional ancestors would cause Jesus to be disqualified from messiahship, but He not only receives murderers in His family, He calls some of them to be His apostles.

- According to Galatians 1:13–16, how did God change this famous persecutor into a New Testament writer?

_____

_____

_____

You may reason, "I am glad Christ welcomes murderers; they are the ones who need forgiveness, not me. I've never murdered anybody." Did you know that according to God's standards, any time you direct sinful anger at someone you commit murder in your heart? Jesus confirms,

> You have heard that the ancients were told, "YOU SHALL NOT COMMIT MURDER" and "Whoever commits murder shall be liable to the court." But I say to you that everyone who is angry with his brother shall be guilty before the court; and whoever says to his brother, "You good-for-nothing," shall be guilty before the supreme court; and whoever says, "You fool," shall be guilty enough to go into the fiery hell (Matthew 5:21–22).

Shockingly, our Majestic Savior welcomes our kind in His family. But according to His genealogy, Christ receives other types of repentant sinners too.

JESUS WELCOMES ADULTERERS

Bathsheba didn't murder anybody, but she partook in David's sin. Even though she had no choice in responding to a royal summons, she should have upheld the purity of her marriage and reminded David of the sanctity of the institution, even if doing so would have cost her life or freedom. The king's mistress would have known the story of Joseph, the patriarch (the son of Jacob, whose biography starts in Genesis 37), who ran from sexual sin when the wife of Potiphar made an advance.

Bathsheba lost the baby from this adulterous liaison, but God gave her another son by David, Solomon, whose name means "peace," contrary to his father, who was a man of war. God made him the wisest man who ever lived, second only to his greater Descendant.

One day, some religious people brought a woman caught in adultery to Christ to see whether He would honor the Mosaic Law, which prescribed death by stoning. He challenged them, "He who is without sin among you, let him be the first to throw a stone at her" (John 8:7). By this standard, He would have been the only one qualified to execute the woman, but instead He showered her with grace: "I do not condemn you, either. Go. From now on sin no more" (John 8:11).

You may reason, "I am glad Jesus welcomes adulterers; they, not I, need forgiveness. I've always been faithful to my spouse." Did you know that according to God's standards, when you look at someone with lust, you commit adultery in your heart? The Majestic Savior alerts, "You have heard that it was said, 'YOU SHALL NOT COMMIT ADULTERY'; but I say to you that everyone who looks at a woman with lust for her has already committed adultery with her in his heart" (Matthew 5:27–28).

Who among us hasn't committed adultery in our heart? I am glad Jesus welcomes our kind in His family. He showers His grace on yet another group of undeserving transgressors who come to Him.

JESUS WELCOMES IDOLATERS

Abraham, the first name of the descending genealogy, which starts in Matthew 1:2, received the promises of progeny, land, and universal blessing (see Genesis 12). His place in this list demonstrates that Jesus is the descendent in whom all the families of the earth will be blessed (Galatians 3:16). Abraham, a giant in the faith, is not there because of alleged perfection, but only by the grace of God, who called him into a covenant relationship while the father of Isaac was still an idolater in the city of Ur of the Chaldeans. But even more shocking, Jesus not only receives idolaters in His family, He transforms them into examples of moral excellence.

Take Ruth, for example. She worshiped Chemosh, the god of Moab, before God assimilated her into the community of Israel through a kinsman redeemer. Her entire blood line came from an incestuous relationship between Lot and one of his daughters (Genesis 19:37). As a result, God cursed that entire nation.

- Read Deuteronomy 23:3, and paraphrase God's curse on the Moabites. Also read the entire book of Ruth and describe divine kindness.

Such undistinguished ancestors would have disqualified Jesus from being the Messiah, you would conclude. But thankfully, He not only receives idolaters in His family, He equips them to be His faithful representatives in sinful societies.

- How does Paul describe the believers in Thessalonica, according to 1 Thessalonians 1:7–9?

You may say, "I am glad Jesus receives idolaters; they need forgiveness. I am not one of them; I don't bow down before idols." According to God's standards, we commit idolatry whenever anyone or anything takes the place of God in our hearts. Again, I direct you to the words of Christ: "YOU SHALL LOVE THE LORD YOUR GOD WITH ALL YOUR HEART, AND WITH ALL YOUR SOUL, AND WITH ALL YOUR MIND" (Matthew 22:37).

Like me, have you ever worshiped at the altar of self-aggrandizement, replaced service to God with personal comfort or burned incense to your own achievements? We should be thankful Jesus welcomes our kind in His family. Amazingly, according to the genealogy in the prologue of the Gospel of Matthew, one more unimpressive bunch receives His kindness.

JESUS WELCOMES FORNICATORS

Genesis 38 chronicles the infamous story of Tamar, who seduced Judah. Not wanting to wait for her promised husband to mature into adulthood, she resorted to harlotry with her father-in-law. The patriarch, equally guilty, should have left a better legacy to his descendants.

The next woman in the list in Matthew 1:1–17, Rahab the Canaanite prostitute, sheltered Jewish spies during the invasion of Jericho, under the leadership of Joshua. She made it to the messianic line and, according to Hebrews 11:31 and James 2:25, abandoned her way of life by divine enablement.

The following pattern emerges in Jesus's genealogy: He not only receives fornicators in His family, He renews them as if they had never sinned.

- Read 1 Corinthians 6:9–11, and list the types of sexual sinners God saves.

Not all of us have committed fornication, but we have friends and family who lead a lifestyle that dishonors God. We should be glad Christ receives repentant sinners in His family.

The last ancestress in the genealogy of Christ deserves attention, not because of any particular sinful pattern, but because by clarifying that Jesus is not the natural son of Joseph, Matthew alludes to the virgin birth, which he describes in the next portion of the narrative.

Although Scripture records no example of iniquity in Mary's life, she admits to being a sinner. Luke records her words in the song known as the *Magnificat*: "My soul exalts the Lord, and my spirit has rejoiced in God my Savior" (Luke 1:46–47). Only sinners need a Savior. Even though Christ's imperfect mother deserves to be admired, she should not be worshiped.

Sinners populate Jesus's family line, but "where sin increased, grace abounded all the more" (Romans 5:20). We could nickname this genealogy "Jesus the friend of sinners." By starting his Gospel with this royal ancestry, Matthew demonstrated Christ's kingly and Savior credentials. Our Majestic Savior not only adopts repentant sinners into His family, He transforms us.

One day Ron Blankley saw a student reading the Bible on the campus of the University of Pennsylvania. He approached the young man and asked what text he was reading. The student showed him the genealogies of Christ in Matthew and Luke but admitted being confused and discouraged because they seemed contradictory. Blankley was a member of Tenth Presbyterian Church in Philadelphia, where James Montgomery Boice had preached from Matthew 1:1–17 weeks before. With permission from the student, Blankley explained the passage and led the man to salvation in Christ.[2] No eloquence or superb reasoning accomplished this. The power of the text, a God-inspired list of names, led that man to His Revered Majesty.

---

2. James Montgomery Boice, *The Gospel of Matthew: The King and His Kingdom, An expository Commentary*, vol. 1 (Grand Rapids, MI: Baker, 2001), 19.

A MIRACULOUS ADVENT

(MATTHEW 1:18–25)

We use the word *miracle* loosely these days. Along with *love, awesome,* and *like* (a teenager's favorite), the term has lost its original meaning. We have blurred the distinction between the surprising and the supernatural, between marvelous and miraculous. As a result, we confuse the impossible with the improbable.

Consider the following examples. Finding a parking space in a crowded mall during the Christmas season may be unlikely but can be explained by natural means; it belongs in the category "divine intervention without a miracle." The reversal of a bad diagnosis could be caused by God's answer to prayer, perhaps by miraculous means but not necessarily. He still works through the hands of capable physicians.

On the other hand, the conception of a baby without a human father cannot happen naturally; it qualifies as a miracle because it demands the temporary disruption of the natural order. The virgin birth of Christ serves as the only example in history.

Matthew begins his description of the incarnation of Jesus using words every parent dreads: "This is how you were born." The evangelist needs to preface the account this way because the proper understanding of the miraculous conception of the Messiah is essential to Christianity. No one can claim legitimate, saving faith while denying the virgin birth of Christ. Without it, Jesus would not be divine; His human father would have transferred a sin nature to Him via natural conception. Churches would be nothing more than social clubs. Gathering on Sundays to celebrate Him would constitute a monumental waste of time and resources, because He would not have risen from the dead. Therefore, solidifying this doctrine in your heart and mind will not only strengthen your faith in Christ and boost your confidence in the Word of God, it will also lead you home in turbulent times.

- According to Galatians 4:4–5, how does Paul relate Jesus's incarnation with God's ability to save?

- How would you describe Christ's dual nature (human and divine) according to the following passages?

Colossians 1:15–20:

_____

_____

_____

_____

Hebrews 1:1–3:

_____

_____

_____

_____

Luke also records the supernatural conception of Jesus but from Mary's perspective and with the interest of a historian and a physician. Matthew gives us Joseph's viewpoint.

- Read Matthew 1:18–25, and describe how the scene elaborates on Matthew 1:16.

_____

_____

_____

_____

To understand how the virgin birth portrays the revered majesty of Christ, let's break up His miraculous advent into five parts.

A GODLY CONCEPTION

Remember, because Matthew's original readers are Jewish, he does not feel the need to explain local marriage customs. He places Mary and Joseph in the narrative already in the betrothal phase of their relationship. The parents of the bride and the groom would have already arranged their marriage, and Joseph's father would have paid the dowry to compensate Mary's father for the ceremony. Depending on their financial situation, the family of the bride would have held the money in a trust in case the husband died unexpectedly.

After the negotiations, Joseph and Mary were considered husband and wife (legally married) but would have abstained from physical intimacy until after the wedding feast. During this time each spouse would have remained with his and her parents to prove faithfulness to one another and until the groom finished building the house.

Jesus borrowed this imagery when He comforted the disciples with the promise of His return: "In My Father's house are many dwelling places; if it were not so, I would have told you; for I go to prepare a place for you. If I go and prepare a place for you, I will come again and receive you to Myself, that where I am, there you may be also" (John 14:2–3).

- Describe Joseph's dilemma according to Matthew 1:18.

Did Mary have an affair with a Roman soldier? Was she raped? Years later, when Jesus confronted the hypocrisy of some religious leaders, they articulated the first attack on the doctrine of Christ's virgin birth: "We were not born of fornication; we have one Father: God" (John 8:41). With these words they accused Jesus's mother of adultery, which would have made Him an illegitimate son, while advertising their Jewish pure-bloodedness. But Matthew purposefully notes that Mary remained a virgin until the birth of Her Majestic Firstborn.

Luke fills in the details about Mary's discovery of her miraculous pregnancy. He complements (and would never contradict) Matthew's account.

- Read Luke 1:26–33, and harmonize it with Matthew's description of the virgin birth.

A GODLY CLARIFICATION

Matthew highlights a character quality in Joseph. The adopted father of Jesus suspected Mary had been unfaithful, a crime that would have been punished by death by stoning, according to the Mosaic Law (Deuteronomy 22:23–34). He did not want to expose his wife to public shame, but driven by godliness, he realized he could not proceed with the betrothal. Out of compassion, he planned to dissolve the engagement quietly, which would have required two witnesses. Formal divorce proceedings done privately involving the two families would have begun, Mary's bump on her belly providing an easy case for annulment. They would have canceled the marriage supper and made financial restitutions. But even with a broken heart, Joseph had the nobility of character to withhold revenge.

Most of us would have broadcast the wrongdoing we suffered, claimed victimhood, and sought retaliation. Not the adopted father of our Majestic Savior. He was not sinless, of course, but Scripture wants us to know that the unique ministry for which God called this man required the highest level of unassuming, quiet, and humble integrity. Notice that in the Bible he is never called "the father of Jesus" but always "the husband of Mary."

God comforted Joseph by clarifying the matter through extraordinary means. Because the apparent unfaithfulness troubled his heart and mind, the husband of Mary would have dreamed about it (just like we dream about issues that trouble us, especially if we think about them before bed). But his unusual experience came from above, not his own heart. The angel who visited Joseph in his dream was real, but perhaps God put him to sleep to prevent panic when seeing the heavenly messenger. Because no one had ever called Joseph by the title "son of David," the angelic announcement brought clarification, relief, and amazement to him. He "put two and two together" and realized his life would never be the same.

A GODLY COMMAND

The angel also instructed Joseph what to name the child, which confirmed the heavenly instruction to Mary, according to Luke. "Jesus," the Greek rendition of "Joshua" (*Yeshua*), means "Yahweh saves."

- Read Psalm 130. How would Matthew's Jewish audience connect verse 8 with the angelic announcement?

The expression "His people" refers to the Jews, but in the next scene Matthew reports that gentiles, the magi, worshiped Jesus. Therefore, while Jesus came to save the Jews, He also includes non-Jews in His redemptive plan.

Let's follow Matthew's lead and look at this story from the perspective of Joseph. Unplanned fatherhood would have brought several inconveniences to him, evidenced by the fact that he had to move to Bethlehem for the birth of the baby and settle back in Nazareth. Essentially, God called Joseph to sacrifice self-interest and serve our King in a unique and non-repeatable way. This ordinary carpenter would have the unfathomable joy and privilege to raise the Messiah. Thankfully, when you parent the God-Man, there are no "terrible twos," no temper tantrums, no teenager rebellion, no time-outs, no "one week without TV," no "hand over your cell phone." Imagine Joseph reading the Old Testament to Jesus. How do you teach the written Word to the Living Word?

Joseph sacrificed his reputation for God. He didn't even get to name his stepson. Can you imagine the gossip, ridicule, and sarcasm from others? People in the community would mock him: "Joseph, do you really believe this story about the power of the Almighty overshadowing your wife? Tell us, what Roman military base has she visited?" Because he wanted to protect Mary from public shame, he would have shielded her from criticism and borne all the insults himself. Being a godly man, he would have used the virgin birth as an opportunity to share the gospel with his mockers.

Joseph also sacrificed his comfort for the Lord. Egypt has always represented hostility toward the people of God. After the birth of Christ, the family had to flee there, the obvious choice because the false king of the Jews, Herod, wanted to kill the true Monarch. After the death of the usurper, they relocated to a city despised even by their countrymen.

- According to John 1:46, why did Nathanael seem surprised to learn that the Messiah grew up in Nazareth?

_____

_____

_____

Scripture gives us no indication that Joseph turned bitter or rebelled against God. Although this story is not about him, Mary's husband personifies a Christ-centered life, the opposite of the self-centeredness so common in our time. His place in God's redemptive plan is unique, but we share with him the high calling to sacrifice for our Majestic Savior. If you are a Christian, just like Joseph, you belong to the family of Christ by grace through faith. Jesus calls you to be His imitator, an endeavor that demands crucifixion of self (Matthew 16:25). But you will also find your way home in turbulent times.

- Read Colossians 2:20, and list ways in which Christ manifests His life in you.

_____

_____

_____

Forgive me for disappointing you, dear reader, but the Christian life is not about you. The gospel knows nothing about pursuing worldly success, achieving personal dreams, finding a soulmate, or seeking self-fulfillment. These are popular but grotesque distortions of the message God called us to preach. I have seen people "make shipwreck of their faith" (to borrow an expression from Paul in 1 Timothy 1:19) because they fail to read their Bibles carefully and, as a result, misunderstand the cost of following Christ.

Jesus is not a life coach, shrink, guru, or a genie in a bottle. He is the Majestic Savior who died in the place of sinners and now offers us eternal life. Salvation is a free gift from God, but following Him will cost us greatly (just like it cost Joseph). We cannot simultaneously pursue personal glory _and_ His command to make disciples; one cancels the other. Both projects will consume our energy and resources—we can only give our lives to the pursuit of one of them. Many Christians choose the former, which epitomizes shortsightedness. Seeking personal glory may produce admiration from people, but the feeling of accomplishment will fade like vapor. Chasing Christ's project, on the other hand, produces eternal, incorruptible rewards.

- How does Jesus summarize the cost of discipleship according to Matthew 10:38–39?

_____

_____

_____

- According to John 6:60, how does John describe the response from some of Christ's disciples when they heard of the high cost of following Jesus? How have you responded?

- List heavenly rewards according to the following passages.

  James 1:12:

  2 Timothy 4:8:

  1 Peter 1:3–4:

  1 Peter 5:4:

  Revelation 2:12:

Admittedly, the command to die to self confronts our self-preservation instincts. Our flesh rises in rebellion against it, yet these words are the perfect wisdom from Christ. Why do you think preachers avoid this topic? I may not like them, but by faith and with His enabling grace I will trust Him who knows better.

Are you willing to let God interfere in your plans to accomplish His purposes? Are you ready to lay down your dreams to pursue His? He will not call you to raise the Messiah, but He may call you to give up a comfort and convenience so that you can pursue anonymity for Him, like Corrie Ten Boom, the self-described tramp for the Lord,[3] or Paul, an under-rower (the galley slave in a Roman warship [1 Corinthians 4:1]).

Scripture says almost nothing about Joseph after this, proving the point that he existed to exalt Christ, not self.

A GODLY CONFIRMATION

The first Old Testament passage Matthew quotes in his Gospel is Isaiah 7:14. Here he links the conception of Christ with the fulfillment of the prophecy about the virgin birth and refutes common myths at the time about other supposed virgin births.

Some people like to point out that the Hebrew word for "virgin" in the Isaiah passage refers to a young woman or a maiden but not necessarily one who has never been with a man. Granted, the word can mean "a young woman," but the Gospel writer, inspired by God, opens and closes this portion of the book by clarifying that the young woman was also a [parthenos (v. 23), translated literally as "virgin."

Mary herself confirmed her virginity when she asked the angel in Luke's account of the announcement: "How can this be, since I am a virgin?" (1:34). (Or: "I have not known a man."

The name Immanuel describes a messianic designation, God in human flesh.

- How does John explain this concept in John 1:14?

- How does Jesus explain it in John 10:30?

---

3. Corrie Ten Boom, *Tramp for the Lord: The Unforgettable True Story of Faith and Survival* (New York, NY: Berkley, 1974).

- How does Paul explain it in Colossians 2:9?

God with us is the God who lived for us in order to die for us, but sadly, for people who reject Christ, He will be "God against us." They will spend eternity separated from their Creator and suffering. I can think of no more catastrophic tragedy.

A GODLY COMPLY

Matthew does not reveal anything about the next phase of the betrothal of Joseph and Mary, which would have been the marriage celebration. He does clarify that the physical consummation of their union only took place after the birth of Christ. Evidently, they understood the significance of the virgin birth and did not want to call into question the supernatural conception of Jesus. Someone could have pointed out that Christ was Joseph's natural son and that husband and wife lied about the date of the pregnancy to cover up the alleged sin of fornication.

By the way, their temporary abstinence after marriage is another example of sacrificial service to God. The evangelist does not tell us that the angel instructed Joseph to abstain during the pregnancy. Under his leadership, the couple decided together to wait for the birth of the Messiah, after which they enjoyed the blessings of physical union in marriage. The Bible mentions Mary's children with Joseph born after the birth of Jesus (John 7:5).

The last sentence of Matthew 1 also bears testimony to the godliness of the adopted father of Christ. He obeyed God at great personal cost. He named the Son exactly as the angel instructed him and didn't feel the need to insert his own opinion but understood his place as a steward of the life of His own savior.

Miracles happen today but not the ones fabricated in so-called miracle crusades. According to Ephesians 2:1–7, every time someone comes to faith in Christ a spiritual resurrection takes place, which prefigures a physical resurrection. Our Majestic Savior, born of a virgin to die and conquer the grave on behalf of undeserving sinners, made that possible.

Next, let's meet some wise men who recognized His revered majesty.

A Meaningful Appointment

(Matthew 2:1–12)

An appointment with a cardiologist brings the potential for anxiety. The doctor reveals the condition of the patient's heart and may prescribe lifestyle or dietary changes.

Consider me a secretary calling on behalf of the Great Physician to remind you it's time for a checkup—no need to feel anxious for this one. His scalpel is "sharper than any two-edged sword, and piercing as far as the division of soul and spirit, of both joints and marrow, and able to judge the thoughts and intentions of the heart" (Hebrews 4:12). Ready for your appointment?

After describing the messianic ancestry and the miraculous advent of Christ, Matthew chronicles the meaningful appointment of some wise men with the toddler Jesus. Some of the original readers probably still remembered the mockery of the Roman soldiers placing a crown of thorns on Christ's head.

In the scene immediately following the birth of Christ, Matthew illustrates the universal reach of the gospel. Even though Jesus came to His own, "those who were His own did not receive Him. But as many as received Him, to them He gave the right to become children of God, even to those who believe in His name, who were born, not of blood nor of the will of the flesh nor of the will of man, but of God" (John 1:11–13). The King of the Jews is the King of kings, the God of the universe who became flesh to die for sinners and call people to Himself from "every tribe and tongue and people and nation" (Revelation 5:9).

- How would this meaningful appointment preview what Jesus said in Matthew 8:11?

Matthew highlights distinct responses to the advent of Christ. The three different groups in the narrative represent three attitudes of the human heart. Everyone in this scene shares something in common: they heard of Jesus, and their responses to Him expose their spiritual condition, which ranges from ideal to disastrous. People today have similar heart predicaments. First, when they hear about the Lord some respond in amazement, which produces a humble heart. The wise men from the east symbolize this group.

- Read Matthew 2:1–12, and identify the main and orbital characters as well as their virtues and vices.

"Magi" is the anglicized version of the word *magoi*, a tribe of Persian priests from the time of Daniel. The English language transliterated the word and coined the term magic.

- Read Daniel 2:2, and identify a similar-sounding word. The Septuagint (Greek translation of the Old Testament) uses the word *magoi* in this verse.

These people were not kings, despite what Christmas cards say. They practiced Zoroastrianism and received the title "wise men" because of their perceived ability to discern spiritual mysteries by astrology, divination, and sorcery (all of which the Bible condemns). As a result, rulers consulted them for wisdom and, with time, gave them the designation of makers of kings. (Keep this in mind, and you will understand Herod's concern with the birth of the true Monarch.)

After the conquest of Babylon by the Medes (see Daniel 5:30), Daniel, who had been taken captive several years before, interacted with the ancestors of these wise men. Undoubtedly, the captive's ability to interpret dreams fascinated them. The Jewish prophet's fame circulated among the *magoi*, according to Daniel 6:28: "So this Daniel enjoyed success in the reign of Darius and in the reign of Cyrus the Persian."

Knowing what we know about God's love for all people and Daniel's godliness, we can safely conclude that he led some of them to faith in Yahweh. Their descendants would have learned about the promised Messiah because they had access to the prophet's writings. They would have had a particular interest in Daniel 9:24–25:

> Seventy weeks have been decreed for your people and your holy city,
> to finish the transgression, to make an end of sin, to make atonement
> for iniquity, to bring in everlasting righteousness, to seal up vision and
> prophecy and to anoint the most holy place. So you are to know and discern that from the issuing of a decree to restore and rebuild Jerusalem

until Messiah the Prince there will be seven weeks and sixty-two weeks;
it will be built again, with plaza and moat, even in times of distress.

Fast-forward several centuries to the days of Herod. The descendants of the magi calculated the time of the birth of the Messiah, and with divine assistance in the form of an unusual star, arrived in Jerusalem by the time Jesus was a toddler. Matthew does not tell us how many of them visited Christ. There may have been four or five, or an entire entourage. We assume there were three because of the three gifts they brought, but they were not named Balthazar, Melchior, and Caspar. They could have been Gunther, Frank, and Mario or Dana, Bob, Nolan, and José," although they probably had Persian names.

Let's remember an important principle in Bible interpretation: resist the temptation to fill in the gaps when Scripture withholds information; God provides plenty of spiritual nourishment in the narrative at face value. In the case of the four Gospels, if none of the other evangelists furnish details, we should not volunteer information we don't know.

The magi followed His star, perhaps some manifestation of the glory of God rather than a celestial body. (Imagine the damage to our solar system that a massive star would make by traveling across the visible universe; the gravity pull alone would have shaken the entire Milky Way.)

Luke tells us that when Jesus was born, there were shepherds watching their flock by night.

- Describe the reaction of the shepherds when they saw the glory of God, according to Luke 2:9.

- Compare this type of reaction with what happened to John in Revelation 1:17.

- According to Jesus in the Olivet Discourse, what sign will precede His Second Coming? See Matthew 24:30.

The magi's amazement of the Messiah produced a humble heart, evident by their prostrated position before the Majestic Toddler. They may have been wise men, but at that moment they realized they stood before the all-knowing God in human flesh. They rejoiced exceedingly (Matthew 2:10), and their gifts matched their understanding of Christ's life and ministry. Gold, always associated with royalty in the Bible, highlights the majesty of the Child. Incense symbolizes the priesthood of Christ, who mediates between God and man. Myrrh, used to mask the stench of death, foreshadowed the cross, a pleasant aroma to the Father and an acceptable sacrifice to atone for sins.

Perhaps the magi represent people whose hearts are drawn to Christ after hearing the gospel and recognize their insignificance compared to the greatness of our Savior. The wise men from the east also teach us the application of Proverbs 1:7: "The fear of the LORD is the beginning of knowledge." This fear does not cause terror (although God's holiness frightens sinners), but a reverent respect, a recognition that all wisdom belongs to Him. We should follow their example and prostrate before Christ, not necessarily physically but replicating the same heart attitude of these ancient king makers who recognized Jesus as the Majestic Savior. In an attitude of worship, we must offer Him our best service.

The text reveals another noteworthy reaction of a character, the antagonist. When people hear about Jesus, some respond in amazement, which produces a humble heart, but others respond with a form of animosity that produces hostility.

Herod the Great represents this group. The Roman senate assigned this Edomite (a descendant of Esau) kingship in Judea in 37 BC, but devoid of royal blood, he failed to qualify as king of the Jews. The question from the magi must have enraged the impostor, who didn't kill the wise men in a fit of anger because they had information he needed.

When the usurper heard that a well-known tribe of kingmakers came to Jerusalem to acknowledge the birth of the One who possesses true majesty, Herod worried about the possibility of being discovered as a counterfeit and dethroned. The people of Jerusalem panicked because the fake despot had a notorious anger problem that usually resulted in bloodshed. Although subordinate to Caesar, within his jurisdiction Herod had the autonomy to order executions. The counterfeit king wanted to eliminate any rightful claimant to royalty, so he summoned the Jewish chief priests and scribes to determine the exact residence of the Child, not because he desired to worship Christ, but because he wished to murder Him. His animosity for the Messiah produced a hostile heart.

Like Herod, many people hate Christ today because Jesus inconveniences their sinful lifestyle. They want to remain on the throne of their own lives and would kill Him if they had the opportunity. Satan has successfully deceived them into thinking they are kings and should be treated accordingly. The concept of servanthood troubles them.

Honesty compels us to admit that even Christians struggle with this virtue. We know our "Christianese" well. We don't mind being called servants (we put the title in our email signatures), but we don't like being treated like one. We are not hostile to the kingship of Christ, like Herod, but we must concede that our flesh sometimes resents it. From time to time we face the temptation to push Him off of His throne and say, "Jesus, you got the saving business down, but let me take care of my finances. Never mind the fact that my resources come from you." Or we may tell Him, "Jesus, I'm going to do this marriage thing my way. You were never married; what do you know? I know you commanded us to forgive and to consider others better than ourselves, but that hasn't fulfilled me. I'm going to retaliate." These attitudes expose a serious heart condition called "animosity toward Christ." The Bible prescribes repentance and brokenness before that hard-heartedness turns to enmity.

Let's turn our attention back to the people that Herod represents—the haters of Christ. Because they can't kill Jesus, the only alternative is to silence his Word. They can't do that either, so they persecute His followers, especially the faithful ones who live the truth of Scripture. In our society, the persecutors are not barbarians; they are more sophisticated. Instead of sending us to a Roman arena to be eaten alive by beasts, they use social media to slander and mock Christ and His followers. They also express their hostility through our legal system.

- According to 1 Corinthians 16:13 and Matthew 5:44, how should we respond to this type of antagonism?

- What does it mean to "act like men"? Define biblical manhood.

If people oppose you because you follow Christ, they do it not because of who you are, but because of whose you are. Let Jesus encourage you again: "If the world hates you, you know that it has hated Me before it hated you. If you were of the world, the world would love its own; but because you are not of the world, but I chose you out of the world, because of this the world hates you" (John 15:18–19).

I must note a third type of reaction of people who are exposed to Jesus. Some respond in amazement, which produces a humble heart; others respond in animosity, which produces a hostile heart; but many respond with apathy, which produces a hard heart.

The Jewish chief priests and scribes of Jerusalem at the time represent this group. They should have been expecting the Messiah with joy (if they really understood Old Testament prophecy), like the man whose joy Luke describes:

> And there was a man in Jerusalem whose name was Simeon; and this man was righteous and devout, looking for the consolation of Israel; and the Holy Spirit was upon him. And it had been revealed to him by the Holy Spirit that he would not see death before he had seen the Lord's Christ. And he came in the Spirit into the temple; and when the parents brought in the child Jesus, to carry out for Him the custom of the Law, then he took Him into his arms, and blessed God, and said,

> "Now Lord, You are releasing Your bond-servant to depart in peace,
> According to Your word;
> For my eyes have seen Your salvation,
> Which You have prepared in the presence of all peoples,
> A Light of revelation to the Gentiles,
> And the glory of Your people Israel (Luke 2:25–32).

The scribes, particularly, because they copied manuscripts of God's Law for a living, should have had a similar reaction. In fact, they should have led the pilgrimage to Bethlehem in search of the Messiah.

Matthew paraphrased Micah 5:2 (see Matthew 2:6) by pointing out the fulfillment of Old Testament prophecy. Under divine inspiration, his commentary on messianic prediction solidifies the fact that both testaments reveal Christ. Jesus Himself confirms this: "You search the Scriptures because you think that in them you have eternal life; it is these that testify about Me" (John 5:39).

The indifference of the Jewish leaders turned into rejection, something that the author of the first Gospel clarifies in chapter 12. By the end of the narrative, their hard hearts led them to crucify their own Messiah. They took Him for granted and preferred to keep the façade of religiosity, worshiping God with their lips only while their hearts remained far from Him.

The chief priests and scribes symbolize people who see themselves as self-righteous, folks who believe that they don't need a Savior because they are already good enough to make it to heaven or that they have a better plan apart from the cross. They usually live morally upright, defend good causes, and give to charity, but tragically, they remain separated from God. Contrary to the second group (represented by Herod), this one features passive-aggressive enemies of God. Their hostility to Christ is not immediately obvious but hypocritical. They usually decline affiliation with a local congregation and boldly proclaim, "Alcoholics, murderers, and the sexually depraved need the church. I don't."

This thought process makes sense if you don't want to be identified with a common image Christ uses to refer to His followers. Sheep are fragile animals that need constant supervision and care. Many people prefer being associated with lions and therefore approach

God on their own terms, which usually include an elevated view of self and a low and incorrect view of Christ. These are the people who consider Jesus one option among many to get to the Father. They will come to the Savior as long as He doesn't interfere with their religion of self-worship (which is the sophisticated and modern version of idolatry) or as long as it doesn't cost them anything and they can keep their pet sins.

That hardness of heart alienates people from God. Jesus dealt harshly with the self-righteous of His day.

We should pray that God will soften hard hearts so that the gospel can penetrate the outer layers of self-righteousness and get to the core of our being. I never want my love for Christ to grow cold, to be indifferent toward Him, the most important person of my life. Tragedies, heartbreak, and unmet expectations can squeeze our passion for our precious Savior, a tragedy that has happened to entire denominations. People who were once on fire for Christ have become professional religionists who removed Jesus from His place of prominence. I'd rather die than see this at the church I serve. I hope you share my desire.

In this chapter we identified three groups of people who react in different ways when exposed to Jesus. Which of the groups describes you? According to the last sentence of this scene, the magi returned to their country by another way (v. 12). Matthew refers to a physical journey, of course, but I want to ask you about your spiritual walk. Just like God led the wise men to Jesus by a manifestation of His glory, He leads you to Him today by His Word. He wants you to come home, not by the way of animosity or apathy toward Jesus, but by the path of amazement that leads to worship from a humble and thankful heart. If your heart has hardened toward Christ, I am concerned about your heart condition. But I have good news: He wants to give you a new one. He will do that because He loves you and calls you to Himself. The most meaningful appointment of your life can happen today if you will come to Christ in faith. Let's meet a man who failed to do so, the New Testament's first mass murderer.

A MEAN ANTAGONIST

(MATTHEW 2:13–23)

Norman Geisler once wrote, "The New Testament is in the Old Testament concealed; the Old Testament is in the New Testament revealed."[4] The second half of the second chapter in the Gospel of Matthew demonstrates this idea clearly. In this passage, the writer explains three Old Testament prophecies, which function as signposts that guide us to security in Christ. Primarily, however, Matthew proves that Christianity was not an invention, but the fulfillment of every messianic hope, including the very first one recorded in the Bible, when God sentences the serpent: "And I will put enmity between you and the woman, and between your seed and her seed; He shall bruise you on the head, and you shall bruise him on the heel" (Genesis 3:15). This prophecy provides the biblical background of what we will study in this chapter.

• Read Matthew 2:13–23, and describe how the Bible interprets itself.

The scene narrates a humble start followed by a horrible slaughter and gives us a clear example of the hostility toward the seed of the woman (Jesus) from the part of the seed of the serpent (Satan influencing Herod). The impostor king, unable to control his anger, stages a massacre of infants in Bethlehem to attempt to eliminate the true Ruler.

The Bible interprets itself. Matthew explains at least two Old Testament references in this section, but the connection between testaments goes beyond the fulfillment of prophecy. For example, just like the author of the book of Genesis, the Gospel writer describes a man named Joseph who has dreams and travels to Egypt. Also, like the book of Exodus does, Matthew tells the tale of a king who massacred male babies. These similarities are not coincidental. Obviously, the evangelist wants to show his original readers that Jesus

---

4. Norman L. Geisler, *A Popular Survey of the New Testament* (Grand Rapids, MI: Baker Books, 2007), 10.

fulfills every messianic hope prophesied in the Word of God, as if he were saying: "How could you have missed your Messiah? He is all over our Scriptures."

Likewise, the text warns us to not miss Jesus. Not only does He fulfill every messianic promise, He meets every need of the human heart. In order to demonstrate this, allow me to break up this scene into small parts based on geography, since every prophecy Matthew invokes in this passage concerns a location described in the Old Testament.

THE SOJOURN IN EGYPT

The author brings Joseph back to the narrative. By now, Jesus's stepfather has grown used to angels talking to him in dreams. This time the heavenly messenger reveals Herod's intentions. Thankfully, God knew the heart of the evil king before the madman ordered the infanticide. Joseph, being a godly man (we verified that in chapter 2 of this book), obeyed as soon as he woke up.

Although this is not the main point of the passage, we cannot skip another valuable lesson from the adopted father of the Messiah. He followed the divine instructions immediately—no questions asked, no arguing with God or demanding more information. Godly people usually respond like him to God's Word. They moved as soon as He made His expectation clear, even if that expectation involved a temporary inconvenience or hardship (such as getting up in the middle of the night for an unplanned trip).

What does God expect of you? If you don't know, don't expect a dream; He placed the answer in the book your pastor (hopefully) preaches every Sunday. But I will give you one hint: if you're a married man, he wants you to love your wife sacrificially. If you're a married woman, he wants you to love your husband and submit to his leadership. (Look at Ephesians 5.) By the way, married couples will always do well to follow the examples of Joseph and Mary.

Matthew explains the event commonly known as the flight to Egypt, the obvious choice because the land of the pharaohs, although a Roman province at the time, did not fall under Herod's jurisdiction. Many Jews had settled there (in Alexandria, specifically) during the period between testaments.

I heard the story of a Sunday school teacher who asked the children in her class to sketch this scene. One of the kids drew an airplane with four people in the cockpit. Mrs. Bennet, the teacher, asked, "What's an airplane doing here, and who are these people?"

Little Jimmie responded, "Jesus, Joseph, and Mary on the flight to Egypt."

Attempting to contain her laughter, Mrs. Bennet asked, "Who's the fourth one?"

"That's Pontius, the pilot."

Matthew does not tell us how Jesus, Joseph, and Mary fled to Egypt, though they probably rode a camel. Instead, he clarifies that although Hosea 11:1, the first Old Testament reference he quotes in this passage, speaks of the exodus, the picture points to Christ.

Commentators call this feature of the Bible a type. The image would have stirred hope of deliverance in the hearts of the original readers. They would have associated their bondage under Rome with their ancestors' slavery in Egypt followed by a miraculous redemption. By drawing the parallel, Matthew reminds us that the exodus generation had a deliverer, but now someone greater than the lawgiver has arrived. Moses freed people from Pharaoh; the Son of God frees people from sin. Thus, Matthew's commentary on this prophecy assures us that Christ alone meets the human need for true freedom.

You may argue and say, "I am an American. I was born free." Yes, we have fought wars to secure political freedom, a basic human longing. But how much more should we desire spiritual freedom? According to the Bible, every one of us is born in bondage of sin, the despot that controls and condemns. We can't do anything about it . . . unless the Son of God sets us free.

- How does Jesus clarify real freedom, according to John 8:36?

Only Christ meets our need for true deliverance. Unless and until people come to Him, they remain chained by the condemnation and control of their iniquities. But Jesus meets another basic human need. By pointing out the Father–Son relationship between God and Jesus, Matthew teaches us that only our Majestic Savior satisfies our craving for true belonging. He alone has the authority to adopt people into the family of God.

- How do people become children of God, according to the following passages? What are the results of belonging to His family?

John 1:12–13:

1 John 3:1:

Romans 8:15:

_____

_____

_____

_____

Galatians 6:10:

_____

_____

_____

_____

From the day of our birth we desire this level of acceptance, and we continue to look for it until we find welcoming arms. Sadly, people find belonging in a gang, a political party, or a cult. But God provided for that basic human need in Christ. Our Majestic Savior calls people to be a part of His family and will not turn anyone away who comes to Him in faith. Even if your parents, children, siblings, or a spouse abandoned you, Jesus will not, because He promised:

> My sheep hear My voice, and I know them, and they follow Me; and I give eternal life to them, and they will never perish; and no one will snatch them out of My hand. My Father, who has given them to Me, is greater than all; and no one is able to snatch them out of the Father's hand. I and the Father are one (John 10:27–30).

You're not going to find true acceptance in a guild, a union, or an association, but in the One who has reminded us: "I am the way, and the truth, and the life; no one comes to the Father but through Me" (John 14:6).

According to Matthew's commentary of Hosea 11:1, Jesus fulfills messianic hopes. Because Christ is the Son of God who sojourned with his parents in Egypt to fulfill the prophecy, He alone meets our needs of spiritual freedom and true belonging. We can stop looking for these blessings in the wrong places.

THE SLAUGHTER IN BETHLEHEM

Matthew associates Herod's genocide with another Old Testament prophecy. Before that, however, he gives us a glimpse into the cruelty of the pagan ruler. The despot with an anger problem ordered this massacre as an overreaction to clear divine instructions to the magi (see Matthew 2:12). Herod did not know that God warned them to take a different route home, but he vowed to make every family with a male child under the age of two pay for his frustration. Just to be sure no one escaped his wrath he included the surrounding villages in his murderous campaign, which was literally overkill. Clearly, his message was: "Don't ever try to cross me. I am the only king in this place. I will not make room for Jesus in this town, much less in my heart."

Matthew clarifies that although an evil man plotted this, the book of Jeremiah had foretold the event (see Jeremiah 31:15), in a verse that reads more like a statement of fact. (In other words, we only know that Jeremiah 31:15 is a prophecy because the Gospel writer tells us.) The passage speaks of the Babylonian captivity in 586 BC.

Once again Scripture presents us with a type, an event that points to the life of Christ through imagery. The image of the matriarch of Israel weeping symbolizes the exile of the nation (the captives would assemble in Ramah to be taken to Babylon and Assyria) but ultimately points to the slaughter in Bethlehem. Surprisingly, however, even in a scene of bloodshed, Jeremiah and Matthew paint a picture of hope.

- Read Jeremiah 31:15–16, and pay close attention to the last sentence.

"Where is the hope in this scene of infanticide?" you may ask.

After the Babylonian captivity, the Jews had no more kings because every male in the royal line lived under the oppression of a foreign power. The period of mourning, symbolized by Rachel's tears, would last from that time until the slaughter in Bethlehem. But now the true King had arrived and escaped death, evident by the fact that Herod could not touch Him. (Thirty-three years later He would defeat death.) Israel will one day return to her land under the benevolent rule of the King of kings.

"I still cannot associate anything positive with the slaughter of babies," you might observe. I share your hesitation. Consider the following thought: each time a Roman soldier snatched a toddler from a desperate mother and pierced his little heart with a sword, the child went immediately to heaven, the same destination of every sacrificed, aborted, or miscarried baby throughout human history. I offer this comfort to you because the Bible is clear about the eternal destiny of babies who die before they are cognitively capable of rejecting Christ.

Examine the following examples:

Second Samuel 12:23 says, "But now he has died; why should I fast? Can I bring him back again? I will go to him, but he will not return to me." These words came from David as he mourned his deceased infant son. He found comfort in knowing he would meet him again in heaven. The man after God's own heart could not be referring to the grave because no one finds comfort in going there.

Jonah 4:11 tells us, "Should I not have compassion on Nineveh, the great city in which there are more than 120,000 persons who do not know the difference between their right and left hand, as well as many animals?" God utters these words in rebuke to Jonah because of the prophet's lack of compassion for sinners. The Lord clarifies that His special grace extends to people who don't have the mental capacity to reject the offer of salvation.

In Jeremiah 19:4–7 we read:

> Because they have forsaken Me and have made this an alien place and have burned sacrifices in it to other gods, that neither they nor their forefathers nor the kings of Judah had ever known, and because they have filled this place with the blood of the innocent and have built the high places of Baal to burn their sons in the fire as burnt offerings to Baal, a thing which I never commanded or spoke of, nor did it ever enter My mind; therefore, behold, days are coming," declares the LORD, "when this place will no longer be called Topheth or the valley of Ben-hinnom, but rather the valley of Slaughter. I will make void the counsel of Judah and Jerusalem in this place, and I will cause them to fall by the sword before their enemies and by the hand of those who seek their life; and I will give over their carcasses as food for the birds of the sky and the beasts of the earth.

God refers to babies sacrificed to pagan gods as innocent, even though children are born with a sinful nature (see Romans 3:23). Newborns don't bypass the cross to get to heaven (no one can); they stand before God as undeserving of divine favor as you and I do, and only receive eternal life on the merit of Christ.

We hope that the bereaved mothers in this scene—victims of the cruelty of an insecure, hateful, satanic man—turned to the One who conquered death for the hope of seeing their children again in heaven, like David. Thus, through a disturbing image, God demonstrates that only Christ fulfills the hope of eternal life. Death, represented by Herod, has no power over Jesus or His followers, or children, used later to exemplify saving faith when He said, "Let the children alone, and do not hinder them from coming to Me; for the kingdom of heaven belongs to such as these" (Matthew 19:14). In a fit of rage, the impostor king murdered these little children, but unknown to him, he sent them immediately to the loving arms of God. If you lost a baby to abortion, miscarriage, accident, or murder, your child awaits you in heaven if you, who have the mental capacity to understand the claims of the gospel, have embraced Jesus as your Savior.

According to Matthew's commentary of Jeremiah 31:15, Jesus fulfills the messianic hope of eternal life and regathering of the redeemed on the earth under the rule of the real King. That's only possible because of the work of the One who defeats death. He is your only hope of eternal life.

THE SETTLING IN NAZARETH

Matthew describes yet another unusual dream by Joseph. Apparently, Herod convinced (or forced) some people to join him in the plot to eliminate Jesus. Joseph's hesitation to move back to Bethlehem, the place of Jesus's birth, is understandable because Archelaus, as bloodthirsty as his father Herod, would have attempted to kill Jesus if he knew the true King had been born.

However, the real reason for Joseph and Mary's settling in Nazareth, Matthew explains, was that God wanted to ensure the fulfillment of another messianic prediction. Because this last reference to prophecy in the passage is not recorded in the Old Testament, it should be viewed as a general understanding among prophets that the Messiah would not have an impressive upbringing by human standards, though He certainly did not have a royal birth. God decided that Christ would spend His early days in a place despised by the Jews precisely to contradict every human definition of greatness.

We crave knowledge. We pay absurd amounts of money for a culturally defined good education. Then we pay more money to have a smartphone so search engines can tell us what we want to know. However, only Jesus meets our need for true wisdom. As His followers, we do not meet any worldly standards of greatness or wisdom. In fact, many people resist coming to Christ because they don't want to be associated with folks who follow an ancient book, which describes a man who claims no one can come to the Father but by Him. As a result, thinking they possess superior wisdom, they prefer to believe in evolution, even though the idea that animals can turn into people comes from fairy tales, like the one about a frog that becomes a prince.

We should not seek the approval of men nor the applause of people. Accolades from the world may boost our self-esteem temporarily, but they collect dust after a while. As Christians, we should abandon any desire to earn the admiration of our society. We identify with Jesus, the unimpressive (by human standards) Nazarene.

- Read Acts 24:5, and identify the pejorative tone used toward the early Christians.

- How does Paul explain this upside-down perspective in 1 Corinthians 1:26–29? What is your claim to insignificance according to worldly patterns?

• Read Mark 9:35, and describe greatness according to God's value system.

_____

_____

_____

_____

Divine wisdom considers lowly, unassuming, unimpressive, despised servants of Christ privileged beyond imagination. We are known not for worldly fame, but for our commitment to the truth, faithfulness, compassion, and kindness. Clearly, through the sojourn in Egypt, the slaughter in Bethlehem, and the settling in Nazareth, Scripture wants us to know that just as Christ fulfills every messianic promise, He meets our basic needs for spiritual freedom, true belonging, salvation from sin, and true wisdom. Now let's meet a man described by Jesus as great.

A MEMORABLE AMBASSADOR

In ancient times, before the official arrival of a king in a city, a forerunner would prepare the way for the monarch, cleaning the roads if necessary. Functioning as a representative, he would alert the people to follow the appropriate protocols for the royal procession of their leader.

In the third chapter of the Gospel of Matthew, the writer introduces the man chosen by God to prepare the way for the people of Israel to welcome the nation's long-awaited Majestic Savior. After the messianic ancestry, a miraculous advent, and a meaningful appointment, we meet a mean antagonist. Now Matthew introduces a memorable ambassador to the narrative. Just like the listeners of John the Baptist needed to make room in their hearts for Christ, we should do the same.

- Read Matthew 3:1–17 in prayerful preparation for today's text, and answer the following questions.

Why does Matthew describe John's wardrobe and diet? See 2 Kings 1:1–8.

What does John mean by the metaphor of God turning stones into children of Abraham?

Why is the image of an ax laid at the root of the trees relevant?

What do you think of John's preaching style? Do we need more or fewer preachers like him today?

• Read Malachi 3:1, and compare it with the scene in Matthew 3.

In the last chapter we studied the narrative by geography for a clearer understanding. Because Matthew now focuses on the forerunner and the Savior, we will follow his lead. Two characters stand out.

THE EXEMPLARY SERVANT

The former tax collector starts the next chapter of his narrative with the inauguration of John's ministry. Luke, the historian and physician, provides the precise chronology. He points out:

> In the fifteenth year of the reign of Tiberius Caesar, when Pontius Pilate was governor of Judea, and Herod was tetrarch of Galilee, and his brother Philip was tetrarch of the region of Ituraea and Trachonitis, and Lysanias was tetrarch of Abilene, in the high priesthood of Annas and Caiaphas, the word of God came to John, the son of Zacharias, in the wilderness. (Luke 3:1–2)

Several years have elapsed between chapters 2 and 3 of the Gospel of Matthew. The writer does not provide background information on the one whose voice cries in the wilderness but simply links his arrival with Old Testament prophecy (Isaiah 40:3), which would have caused Matthew's Jewish audience to associate the baptizer with the ministry of Elijah.

• According to Malachi 4:5, why would Matthew's original readers place John in the prophetic line, along with Elijah?

The readers of this Gospel would have learned that God spoke again through an Elijah-like prophet after four hundred years of silence, the period between testaments. John had priestly lineage but became a prophet by calling. Notably, he exemplified true servant-hood. Let's study his message and the ministry.

His Message

The first time the expression "kingdom of heaven" appears in the Gospels in the baptizer's sermon. Matthew, a Jew, uses this expression as synonymous with "kingdom of God" to avoid using the name of Yahweh casually. The nearness of the kingdom speaks of the arrival of the Majestic Savior, who starts His earthly ministry officially just a few verses later.

Matthew used a specific word to describe John's public ministry. The Greek term for "preaching" refers to a loud proclamation of a herald. Matthew strengthens this idea when he quotes Isaiah 40:3. The baptizer shouted his message in the wilderness to serve a clear purpose—namely, to prepare the hearts of people to receive Christ. To accomplish his purpose, John prefaced his short announcement with a present imperative active verb. "Repent" is not a suggestion or a request; on behalf of God, he commanded people to change their minds. He didn't whisper or ask his listeners: "How do you feel about the kingdom of heaven?" He did not give a TED Talk or lead a roundtable discussion. The Elijah-like prophet issued the summons from the Ruler of the universe.

We need more preachers like him, people of God who are direct, unambiguous, and courageous to herald the Word of God. Too many pastors today tiptoe around the truth, bringing tragic results for the church. I'm afraid we live in the time Paul warned Timothy about: "For the time will come when they will not endure sound doctrine; but wanting to have their ears tickled, they will accumulate for themselves teachers in accordance to their own desires, and will turn away their ears from the truth and will turn aside to myths" (2 Timothy 4:3–4). Sadly, many so-called pastors promote these myths and false teachings.

One of my favorite preachers, Adrian Rogers, once said that the problem with preachers in our time is that nobody wants to kill us anymore. Obviously, the hated baptizer did not fit this category. He made some enemies because he proclaimed the truth, which eventually cost him his life.

His Ministry

Matthew describes John's clothes and lifestyle, which were certainly unusual by today's standards, but Jesus had this to say about his forerunner: "Truly I say to you, among those born of women there has not arisen anyone greater than John the Baptist" (Matthew 11:11). I assure you Christ did not come to this conclusion based on His cousin's sense of fashion, but on the importance of the ministry of preparing the way for the Messiah. What can be more honorable than that? The greatest prophet until that day had this to say about Jesus: "[He] is mightier than I, and I am not fit to untie the thong of His sandals" (Luke 3:16) and "He must increase, but I must decrease. 'He who comes from above is above all, he who is of the earth is from the earth and speaks of the earth. He who comes from heaven is above all'" (John 3:30–31). That's why we call him an exemplary servant. He longed to exalt Christ, fully aware that such a noble goal demanded he bury his desire to draw attention to his own ministry, as important as his preaching was. I have met Christians who desire the opposite, to elevate their own lives above Christ. Sadly, their own plans and dreams take precedence over exalting Jesus.

- Read Matthew 21:25; Acts 13:24; and 19:4, where the word *baptism* appears, and document your initial impressions regarding what the observance accomplished.

_____

_____

_____

John introduces the baptism of repentance in preparation for the reception of Christ. Not to be confused with Jesus's ordinance to the church (see Acts 18:25 and Matthew 28:19) or with ceremonial washings, the baptism of John symbolized an outward expression of an inward change of mind and heart that resulted in a transformed attitude. The baptizer borrowed the symbolism of welcoming gentiles into the community of Israel and commanded it to full-blooded Jews as a picture of a transformed mind. Do you see why people hated him? More clearly, the forerunner of Christ wanted to teach his countrymen that no one can enter the kingdom of heaven by simply belonging to the seed of Abraham, but only by grace through faith in the Messiah, who had finally arrived and offered the kingdom of heaven.

The presence of Pharisees and Sadducees in the scene disturbed John because the two groups were notorious for their outwardly focused religion. He had to use a firm, almost offensive tone. How would you like to be greeted by a preacher by the epithet "brood of vipers"? He did not address the self-proclaimed shepherds of Israel and the aristocrats of his day by "your holiness" "or "your excellency." He assigned to them the title "offspring of Satan." Jesus did the same thing later (see John 8:44). John had in mind desert snakes that look like sticks, who pretended to be something they were not. These stealthy reptiles would stay still until a victim wandered close enough, then they would attack.

The Pharisees were a Jewish sect that formed in the period between testaments. Their name comes from the Hebrew word *parash*, which means "separated." They considered their tradition more authoritative than the Word of God and as a result became zealously hypocritical in their view of the Mosaic Law.

- Read Acts 23:6, and identify a famous Pharisee who came to faith in Christ. Describe his conversion according to Acts 9:1–19.

The Sadducees were a Jewish political party of upper-class citizens also started during the four hundred years between Malachi and John the Baptist. They did not believe in the resurrection of the dead, which caused them to deny the resurrection of Christ three years later. They also denied the existence of angels and demons (Acts 23:8).

- Read Matthew 22:23–33, and describe how Jesus exposed their false belief system.

The Pharisees and the Sadducees did not like each other but were united in their hatred of Jesus; Matthew places them together in several scenes in his Gospel. In anticipation of their objection to the command to bear fruit of repentance (they didn't think they needed repentance), John gives them a bizarre image of God turning stones into children of Abraham. Of course, God would never do this literally. The point of this literary device was to warn the allied enemies of Christ that their religious pedigree had no value for God. The baptizer wanted them to soften their stone-hard hearts by hearing the gracious offer of the kingdom of heaven.

Likewise, many people today have the impression their good works can earn them admission into the kingdom of heaven. They operate by a system of relative goodness that ranks them favorably (perhaps lower than the philanthropist but certainly higher than child molesters and war criminals). However, people's religiosity never impresses God; He looks at the heart, and if Christ is not there, the proverbial tree shows no life and bears no fruit. His only option is to chop it with the ax of judgment. Jesus was about to start offering salvation to those who believe but eternal agony to those who don't.

John, the model preacher, gives us the full picture of Christ, the One who offers grace and at the same time alerts against the danger of unbelief. Let's zoom in on the One John came to announce.

THE EXCELLENT SAVIOR

John finally introduces the One whose way he was born to prepare. The baptizer might have been the greatest man until that day, but he confessed Jesus's supremacy. The Majestic Savior shows up in the narrative in His early thirties, according to Luke's timeline. We will spend the rest of this chapter marveling at His ministry and might.

His Ministry

In his discourse, John contrasts his water baptism with two kinds of baptism Jesus would perform. Before we differentiate the three, we need to understand the meaning of the word *baptism*, the transliteration of the Greek verb *baptizo*. The term means "to dip, sink or immerse." The word paints the perfect picture of what Jesus does with believers now and will do with unbelievers later.

- Read 1 Corinthians 12:13, and identify how Christ places believers into the universal community of the redeemed.

_____

_____

_____

_____

When you came to faith in Christ, the Holy Spirit placed you in the body of Christ. The symbolism refers to the permanent immersing of the new believer in the universal community of New Testament saints. Other than a conviction of sin and gratitude for so great a salvation, we should expect no feelings associated with Spirit baptism because it happens in the spiritual realm. A transformed life, demonstrated gradually, follows this work of God. Therefore, believers don't need to pursue the baptism of the Holy Spirit because God has already baptized—placed—us in Christ.

But John the Baptist also predicted that Jesus would baptize people with fire, a reference to the immersion of unbelievers in eternal judgment. Another John, the revelator, describes the scene of that dreadful day:

> Then I saw a great white throne and Him who sat upon it, from whose presence earth and heaven fled away, and no place was found for them. And I saw the dead, the great and the small, standing before the throne, and books were opened; and another book was opened, which is the book of life; and the dead were judged from the things which were written in the books, according to their deeds. And the sea gave up the dead which were in it, and death and Hades gave up the dead which were in them; and they were judged, every one of them according to their deeds. Then death and Hades were thrown into the lake of fire. This is the second death, the lake of fire. And if anyone's name was not found written in the book of life, he was thrown into the lake of fire. (Revelation 20:11–15)

Holy Spirit baptism and fire baptism produce opposite outcomes. It is easy to confuse the two because the Bible often associates the Third Person of the Trinity with fire, heat, and light. However, the context of the baptizer's message conveys a warning. The fruitless tree and the chaff correspond to the unrepentant Pharisees and Sadducees in the immediate context, and they, in turn, represent people who reject Christ.

What do we learn from the baptizing ministry of Jesus? We should alert people to make room in their hearts for Christ. They should receive Him as Savior and be placed into the family of New Testament saints. Otherwise, fire baptism will result in divine wrath; everybody will be baptized one way or another.

His Might

Many people, including John the Baptist, demonstrate surprise about the reason for the baptism of Jesus. Christ certainly did not need to repent of anything. Thankfully, the Savior clarifies the purpose for the symbolic act: to fulfill all righteousness, to do what is right in God's eyes. By being baptized, Jesus identifies with humanity. Paul explains, "He made Him who knew no sin to be sin on our behalf, so that we might become the righteousness of God in Him" (2 Corinthians 5:21). The imagery of a full immersion followed by someone coming out of the water also foretells the death, burial, and resurrection of Christ, the only means by which people can be saved. We are justified by God (declared righteous) when we place our faith in His death, burial, and resurrection. Again, Paul clarifies, "But God demonstrates His own love toward us, in that while we were yet sinners, Christ died for us. Much more then, having now been justified by His blood, we shall be saved from the wrath of God through Him" (Romans 5:8–9).

Here's something else God wants us to know. By describing what happened after the baptism of Jesus, Matthew presents his readers with a picture of the Triune God. The Father affirms the Son (the author quotes Psalms 2:7), the Holy Spirit "lands" on the Son (the picture of a dove represents Christ's sacrifice), and the Son carries out the Father's redemptive plan.

- Read the following verses, and describe the ministry of the three Persons of the Trinity in the lives of believers today.

1 Corinthians 12:13:

2 Timothy 1:14:

Colossians 1:27:

John 14:10:

_____

_____

_____

_____

Because this scene in the first Gospel features the memorable ambassador's job in preparing people's hearts to receive Christ, I must ask you the obvious question: Have you made room in your heart for Jesus? He will make you as fruitful as the proverbial tree he mentions elsewhere: "I am the vine, you are the branches; he who abides in Me and I in him, he bears much fruit, for apart from Me you can do nothing" (John 15:5).

If you are a believer but someone or something else occupies the throne in your life, today is the day to make the adjustment so that Jesus can take his rightful place. Let's continue to find our way home by uncovering His enemy's plot to destroy both the Revered King and His followers.

A MALICIOUS ADVERSARY

(MATTHEW 4:1–11)

I don't like to begin a chapter describing Satan, but he shows up in the narrative in the fourth chapter of the Gospel of Matthew. Since we've been studying this portion of Scripture in preparation for the Kingdom Parables, we will do well to understand the devil's objectives. The Bible instructs believers to "put on the full armor of God, so that you will be able to stand firm against the schemes of the devil" (Ephesians 6:11). What better way to stand firm than to gather intelligence about our fiercest persecutor in the pinnacle of his campaign against our Majestic Savior? Consider this chapter a reconnaissance flight over enemy-occupied territory. We will learn valuable information about the oppressor's character and mission, as well as how he fights—according to Ephesians 6:16, he throws flaming arrows.

In Matthew 4:1–11 the former tax collector refers to this enemy three times as "the devil," a word translated from the Greek *diabolos*, also "slanderer." Jesus calls him "Satan," a Hebrew term that means "adversary." If Herod was Christ's human antagonist, the devil is the spiritual enemy.

- Describe Satan's strategy according to 1 Peter 5:8.

- Read Matthew 4:1–11, and identify the devil's use of Scripture. List any similarities of strategy that the Sadducees and Pharisees employed years later, in Matthew 22.

This encounter in the wilderness features a dialogue between Christ and Satan and reveals not only Jesus's dual nature as God and man, but also how we can overcome temptation, something we all struggle with daily. Scripture clarifies the nature of our battles: "For our struggle is not against flesh and blood, but against the rulers, against the powers, against the world forces of this darkness, against the spiritual forces of wickedness in the heavenly places" (Ephesians 6:12). This means an invisible enemy has waged war against your soul, and he wants to shame the name of Christ by getting you to commit sin. We're going to look at the threefold strategy from Matthew 4:1–11 to neutralize the attacks of our adversary. We have a record of how he attempted an assault on our Majestic King, but Jesus defeated him as Jesus always does.

Before God's Word debriefs us on our tactic, however, let's look at some preliminary matters that will build the foundation for our strategy.

First, Satan is a real person, not an immaterial force or the personification of evil. He demonstrates the ability to reason, evident in how he interacted with Jesus in this scene. He can influence people and angels and has gathered a following from both created orders (he convinced one third of the angels to join his cause, according to Revelation 12:4). The Bible uses the masculine pronoun to refer to him (the devil is not an "it"), even though he is not a human being but a spirit being; that is, he does not have a body.

Second, although the Bible calls him the tempter (Matthew 4:3; 1 Thessalonians 3:5), the enemy of our souls cannot possibly tempt every believer personally because, as a created being, he has a finite amount of energy and resources. If Satan is not attacking you, it may be because you're serving his purposes without knowing. He will focus on tempting other people.

Third, Satan may be "the prince of the power of the air" (Ephesians 2:2) and "the god of this world" (2 Corinthians 4:4), but he is not omnipresent; God alone possesses this attribute. The devil leads the kingdom of darkness, dispatching lower-ranking demons to do his bidding. His goals include tempting believers, accusing the brethren, and opposing Christ. He wanted to be personally involved in the temptation of Jesus because of the enmity between them prophesied in Genesis 3:15, a Bible verse that troubled Satan throughout the ages but especially when the seed of the woman escaped the wrath of Herod (Matthew 2) and started His earthly ministry. This battle will culminate with the fatal blow to Satan's head that Genesis 3:15 prophesies.

The other reason Satan tempted Christ personally was because each one of the three temptations in Matthew 4 was customized for the God-Man. None of us will ever be tempted to turn stones into bread because we do not have that power. A more fitting temptation would be to steal food rather than work for it and wait on divine providence, which fits exactly with what Satan wants to accomplish: to get Jesus to bypass divine provision.

Consider some other examples of temptations Satan and demons throw at Christians. They all entice us to seek satisfaction outside of God's provision and parameters:

- Seek physical intimacy outside of, or prior to, marriage as designed by God and defined in Scripture, instead of waiting on the Lord.

- Divorce your spouse if you are unfulfilled and chase your happiness at any cost.

- Pursue success in life by cutting corners and being dishonest instead of paying the high price of integrity, generosity, selflessness, and perseverance.

- Lie your way out of trouble and avoid the consequences instead of facing them with repentance and brokenness.

Fourth, Satan and demons cannot read people's minds because they do not possess omniscience—that is, they do not know what you are thinking now. Too many people assign this power to the devil without realizing that spirit beings are limited creatures. We may have the impression that demons can read our thoughts because of the effective communications network from which they operate in the spiritual realm. Data about a targeted person does not necessarily need to travel through physical space. Also keep in mind that Satan and demons have observed human behavior since the Adam and Eve were in the Garden of Eden. They can predict accurately what appeals to "the lust of the flesh and the lust of the eyes and the boastful pride of life" (1 John 2:16).

Fifth, Satan and demons do not have the power to possess inanimate objects, like furniture or appliances. They cannot sabotage the brake system of your car, your stereo, computer, or TV. They certainly influence people to use entertainment for sinful purposes, but there is no need to cast out demons from electronic devices. Just use them for godly purposes. I mention this because I have met people who think they should exorcise their musical instruments before praise band practice. The Bible does not provide any such instructions; a better option is to let our worship flow from a pure heart and a life of godliness.

Sixth, Satan and demons are not the only source of temptation for us. We transfer too much responsibility to the devil because blame-shifting has been a part of human nature since the fall of Adam and Eve. It feels better to say, "The devil made me do it," instead of admitting full responsibility for our actions. Let's not forget Satan's strongest ally is our own sinful nature (aka the flesh). James confirms: "But each one is tempted when he is carried away and enticed by his own lust. Then when lust has conceived, it gives birth to sin; and when sin is accomplished, it brings forth death" (James 1:14–15). Satan partners with our flesh, through his demons, to get us to sin.

The similarities between Christ's temptation and our temptations end in the discussion about human sinful nature. As a perfect man devoid of sin, Jesus never could have committed any iniquity, although Satan's attacks were real. We shouldn't determine our theology (in this case, the impeccability of Christ) on the actions of someone the Bible calls "the father of lies" (John 8:44). Evidently, the devil knows parts of Scripture, but he is not the brightest theologian.

Seventh, Christ identifies with sinners, something evident not only from the account of His baptism (Matthew 3:13–17), but from what the author of the book of Hebrews observes: "For we do not have a high priest who cannot sympathize with our weaknesses, but One who has been tempted in all things as we are, yet without sin" (Hebrews 4:15). Never forget this: Jesus, the friend of sinners, knows how it feels to be tempted to break fellowship with God. Therefore, He is the only One who can truly say to you at every level, "I know how you feel."

- Read Romans 7:14–25, and describe Paul's battle with sin. This elaborates on what God told Cain after the first murder in history: "Sin is crouching at the door; and its desire is for you, but you must master it" (Genesis 4:7).

God took the initiative in the temptation of Christ, demonstrating His complete sovereignty. The Holy Spirit led Jesus to this encounter, obviously not against the will of Jesus—that is, He didn't go kicking and screaming but "was full of the Spirit" (Luke 4:1). Why did the Lord lead His Son to be tempted? Doesn't James 1:13 state, "for God cannot be tempted by evil, and He Himself does not tempt anyone"? This devilish encounter in the wilderness was a test meant to affirm Christ's messianic suitability as well as demonstrate His sinless nature. Jesus is God's beloved Son in whom the Father is well pleased; therefore, sin has no power over Him. He is the only one qualified to die on the cross on behalf of sinners. The wilderness experience was not the only time the enemy attempted to derail Christ's redemptive plan. Our Majestic Savior rebuked Peter sharply with the words, "Get behind me, Satan," when the well-meaning disciple tried to dissuade him from enduring suffering, according to Matthew 16:23.

God wants us to know that because Jesus overcame temptation, we can experience the same victory. Chapters 2 and 3 of Revelation use the expression *overcomer* often to refer to believers. Because of Christ's work on the cross, we are no longer slaves to the control and condemnation of sin.

The devil only acts under divine supervision. He has temporary and restricted autonomy. The malicious adversary is not Christ's coequal; I am not sure we can say Satan is Jesus's archenemy, because that word implies similar capabilities, only on opposite sides. Nevertheless, blinded by pride, Satan thought that he could get Jesus to sin, just like he did with Eve in the Garden of Eden. (Remember, Eve did not have a sinful nature when she talked with the serpent.) The devil's thought process may have gone something like this: "I corrupted sinless humanity. Now it's my chance to corrupt divinity and outsmart God."

The timing of the temptation, in the beginning of Christ's earthly ministry, is significant. Since Satan had failed to kill the toddler Jesus at the hands of Herod, he thought he could sabotage God's plan of redemption by disqualifying Jesus from being the Majestic Savior. That's how much the devil hates people.

Consider Jesus's threefold strategy for how we can overcome temptation.

- Read Matthew 4:4, 7, and 10, and identify the common element in the scene.

_____

_____

_____

In preparation for battle against temptation, memorize the following verses.

Galatians 5:16

1 Peter 5:5

2 Peter 1:3

2 Peter 3:18

REMEMBER THE PROFITABILITY OF GOD'S WORD

Three of the four Gospels include the temptation narrative. Because none of the evangelists witnessed the event, they had to rely on direct revelation from God. Matthew, Mark, and Luke are called synoptic Gospels because they focus on the humanity of Christ. The first Gospel notes that Christ became hungry after fasting for forty days. Because Jesus was about to face the devil head on, He needed the kind of strength you can only get by spending undivided time with the Father, even at the expense of His temporary physical needs. He did not neglect His own health; rather, Jesus applied what He said in John 4:34: "My food is to do the will of Him who sent Me and to accomplish His work." The Father allowed the devil to tempt Christ, to demonstrate to us our Lord's qualification as Majestic Savior.

Jesus's wandering in the wilderness for forty days and forty nights reminded Matthew's original readers of the forty years that the exodus generation spent in the desert. That connection refers to the evangelist's quote of Hosea 11:1, "Out of Egypt I called My Son" (Matthew 2:15). Christ Himself draws this parallel by quoting three times from the book of Deuteronomy. Matthew's point in arranging this scene like he did emerges clearly. God tested the faithfulness of Israel in the desert, but they failed. The One who never fails has made His dwelling among us. Therefore, we can understand His long fast, not necessarily as a model for us to follow, but to clarify Jesus's superiority as the ultimate example of faithfulness. The lesson is simple: Keep your eyes on Christ, not on people, who will always disappoint.

The New Testament does not command fasting for believers but does not condemn it either. We can honor God by abstaining from something good and essential (food, for example) to focus on the Bread of Life (John 6:35). By doing so, you will express your hunger and thirst for righteousness (Matthew 5:6). Just don't do it hypocritically, like the Pharisees of Matthew 6:16. If you are not healthy enough to abstain temporarily from nourishment, choose something else such as entertainment, and be sure your spouse is in total agreement. (You shouldn't be doing anything without your spouse's knowledge anyway, except buying him or her a surprise gift.)

- According to 1 Corinthians 7:5, how does Paul instruct and regulate one type of abstinence that resembles fasting?

Satan appeared in the desert taking some form of physical manifestation. We do not know what he looked like, but he probably did not resemble the cultural appropriation of his features. For example, he did not have two horns, did not carry a pitchfork, and was not red. Don't let the mystery of that encounter distract you from the essence of the message. The devil wanted Christ to focus on His momentary necessity rather than on the One who provides every need.

We face this temptation often. For example, the Bible states clearly that "God will supply all your needs according to His riches in glory in Christ Jesus" (Philippians 4:19), and yet we question that truth. When we doubt His promises, in essence, we call God a liar, saying, "Lord, you are either not powerful enough to provide for me, or you don't love me enough to care about me," neither of which is true. He cares deeply about you. Just because you can't differentiate between a real need and a felt need does not mean He doesn't have you covered. We Americans have a distorted view of "basic need." In fact, here's a secret from Paul: "I know how to get along with humble means, and I also know how to live in prosperity; in any and every circumstance I have learned the secret of being filled and going hungry, both of having abundance and suffering need" (Philippians 4:12). He follows this verse up with what is perhaps the most misapplied and abused verse of the Bible: "I can do all things through Him who strengthens me" (Philippians 4:13).

Satan's opening statement in Matthew 4:3 can also be translated, "Since you are the Son of God," obviously referring to the Father's affirmation in the previous chapter, after the baptism of Christ. The devil displayed his notorious arrogance by demanding a magic trick, in essence, saying, "Entertain me. Satisfy my expectation of how the Son of God must act," as if he were in the position to demand signs from Jesus.

If you ever wondered where the practice of claiming miracles from God comes from, wonder no more. We should never demand anything from Christ. Instead, we bow our knees to Him in submission and gratitude for the cross. "By prayer and supplication and thanksgiving let your requests to God be known" (Philippians 4:6–7), not because He needs information, but because we need to articulate trust in our provider and sustainer.

While Satan will never tempt us to turn stones into bread, he may use similar reasoning when enticing Christians to sin. For example, he may develop the following argument:

"Are you really the beloved child of God? Does your Bible say, 'See how great a love the Father has bestowed on us that we might be called children of God?' Then how come you are in this situation? If He really loved you, you wouldn't be sick, unemployed, persecuted, and so on. You've been waiting way too long; you deserve to fulfill all your dreams. Get after your desires." Shockingly, you may hear variations of this thinking from preachers, but we know the mastermind behind this philosophy, do we not?

Three times, the Majestic Savior answered the tempter, "It is written." In the first one Jesus quotes Deuteronomy 8:3 from memory (the part of the Bible we tend to skip, along with the books of Leviticus and Numbers).

- Read Deuteronomy 8:3 in its original context and compare it with 2 Timothy 3:16–17. What is the meaning of the expression "everything that proceeds out of the mouth of God"?

God "breathed out" every word in the original manuscripts of the Bible without bypassing the writing style of the human authors. He saw to it that everything they wrote reflected the very heart of the Lord. Peter articulates the doctrine of inspiration clearly: "For no prophecy was ever made by an act of human will, but men moved by the Holy Spirit spoke from God" (2 Peter 1:21).

I hope you don't miss the glory of this scene in the desert. The incarnate Word uses the inspired Word to silence the tempter and, in the process, teaches us that Scripture sustains us better than food. When you are in a hospital waiting room trying to make sense of devastating news, which do you think will bring more sustenance: a sandwich or a verse like Romans 8:28 ("God causes all things to work together for good to those who love God, to those who are called according to His purpose")? Which will sustain your starving spirit better: a protein bar or Romans 8:38–39 ("For I am convinced that neither death, nor life, nor angels, nor principalities, nor things present, nor things to come, nor powers, nor height, nor depth, nor any other created thing, will be able to separate us from the love of God, which is in Christ Jesus our Lord")? Will a juicy burger feed your undernourished soul like Psalm 43:5 ("Why are you in despair, O my soul? And why are you disturbed within me? Hope in God, for I shall again praise Him, the help of my countenance and my God")? When your sorrow is so intense you can't get out of bed in the morning, you don't need an omelet; you need Isaiah 40:29–31:

> He gives strength to the weary,
> And to him who lacks might He increases power.
> Though youths grow weary and tired,
> And vigorous young men stumble badly
> Yet those who wait for the LORD

Will gain new strength;
They will mount up with wings like eagles,
They will run and not get tired,
They will walk and not become weary.

Because we don't have a divine mind like Jesus, we should memorize Scripture and quote verses when sin crouches at the door, like the psalmist does: "Your word I have treasured in my heart, that I may not sin against You" (Psalms 119:11).

APPLY THE EFFICACY OF GOD'S WORD

The second exchange between Jesus and the devil started with an intriguing phenomenon. Hard to envision, the travel to the pinnacle of the temple in Jerusalem must have happened in the spiritual realm. (Imagine the commotion if the people visiting the temple at the time would have seen this scene.) Whatever kind of teleportation took place, it happened under God's control, the only One able to transport people back and forth from the spiritual and physical realms (which He did to Paul and John) or bend the fabric of space and time that He created.

But let's focus on the dialogue, which starts in verse 5. As a response to Christ's use of Scripture, Satan quoted Psalms 91:11–12, with a little bit of paraphrasing, but he removed these sentences out of their immediate context to get Christ to misapply them. Psalm 91 is about trusting God: "He who dwells in the shelter of the Most High will abide in the shadow of the Almighty. I will say to the Lord, 'My refuge and my fortress, My God, in whom I trust!'" (Psalms 91:1–2). Satan took these verses out of context and tempted Jesus to test God to do something utterly meaningless. The one quoting the psalm is the same who has questioned and twisted the Word of God from the beginning of time. Remember what Satan told Eve: "Indeed, has God said, 'You shall not eat from any tree of the garden'?" (Genesis 3:1), and "You surely will not die!" (Genesis 3:4).

In response, Jesus applied the Bible correctly. He quoted Deuteronomy 6:16, a direct command from God—"You shall not put the Lord your God to the test, as you tested Him at Massah"—and points back to Exodus 17:2–7 when the people of Israel demanded water and complained that God brought them out of Egypt. Even though these words were originally addressed to that generation, Christ highlights the timeless truth. God tests the faithfulness of people, but people should never test Him.

With that in mind, let's go back to Satan's malicious question to Jesus, "if you are the son of God . . ." The Father already affirmed Christ's sonship (the scene of the baptism in Matthew 3). Nothing will ever change that. Jesus's position in the Trinity does not warrant a demand for miraculous protection to satisfy Satan's malevolent curiosity.

We may fall for this temptation and reason: "The Bible says I am not supposed to do this, but I am going to do it anyway because I know God will forgive me." This faulty logic is exactly what Satan wants you to do. He just doesn't tell you about the terrible consequences for you and your family. An approach that honors God would sound like this:

"The Bible says I am no longer a slave to sin. Even though my body craves this iniquity, by the Lord's enabling grace I am going to walk away from it instead of presuming on divine forgiveness."

- Read the following verses and describe how you would defeat the following temptations.

Sexual sin, 1 Corinthians 6:16:

_____

_____

_____

Self-centeredness, Romans 12:3:

_____

_____

_____

Not trusting God, Matthew 6:31–34:

_____

_____

_____

USE THE CLARITY OF GOD'S WORD

Scripture withholds information about how the devil took Jesus to a high mountain, but we know it occurred supernaturally with divine permission. Luke seems to indicate that this happened outside of time as we understand it: "And he led Him up and showed Him all the kingdoms of the world in a moment of time" (Luke 4:5). Once they arrived, the devil told Jesus a half-truth. The beloved physician fills in the details again. The devil said, "I will give You all this domain and its glory; for it has been handed over to me" (v. 6). That temporary authority was given to Satan is a true statement. John writes that "the whole world lies in the power of the evil one" (1 John 5:19). Satan is the god of this world (2 Corinthians 4:4), but the second half of his statement presents problems: he does not have the authority to give kingdoms to whomever he wants. Paul explains why: "Every person is to be in subjection to the governing authorities. For there is no authority except from God, and those which exist are established by God" (Romans 13:1).

Hitler may have been influenced by Satan, but he only rose to power because God determined it. Likewise, the antichrist of the end times will occupy the world's throne temporarily not because Satan wants it, but because God has already established the fact (and even tells us how it will happen).

Daniel interpreted the handwriting on the wall in the feast of Belshazzar. The message read: "'MENĒ'—God has numbered your kingdom and put an end to it. 'TEKĒL'—you have been weighed on the scales and found deficient. 'PERĒS'—your kingdom has been divided and given over to the Medes and Persians" (Daniel 5:26–28).

Clearly, Satan does not have the authority he wants you to think he does. Everything he does must submit to divine approval, something the book of Job demonstrates unmistakably. In a desperate move, the devil didn't even consider the silliness of offering kingdoms to the King of kings. Glory, majesty, and power already belong to Christ. God has already promised Him an everlasting kingdom.

• How do verses like Luke 1:33 and Revelation 5:13 confirm Jesus's authority to reign?

_____

_____

_____

Why would Jesus take something from Satan that the Father already promised Him? Likewise, why would you take something from the devil that God already promised you? Why take temporary satisfaction when Jesus granted you abundant life? Why trade eternal rewards for earthly ones? We take "good things" that Satan and the world offer because we don't want to wait for the best from God. Such cases of instant gratification are epidemic in our culture.

Jesus confirms the clarity of Scripture by paraphrasing Deuteronomy 6:13–14 and linking the temptation with the people of Israel who had failed to worship the Lord exclusively. Matthew's original readers certainly would have remembered the golden calf fiasco (Exodus 32).

Christ concluded the temptation by commanding Satan to leave, which he did "until an opportune time" (Luke 4:13). Jesus refused to perform miracles for the devil, and God fed Him miraculously. The Majestic Savior refused to summon angelic help at Satan's request, and the Father dispatched angels to serve Him. The King of kings refused to take kingdoms from the tempter, and a few verses later He offered the kingdom to people (verse 17). The timeless lesson emerges gloriously from the text: receiving later from God is infinitely better than taking anything from Satan now.

Let's discover Christ's assignment so that we can have a clearer understanding of the kingdom parables.

A MONUMENTAL ASSIGNMENT

(MATTHEW 4:12–25)

The scene in the second half of Matthew 4 reveals important aspects of the character of Christ, upon which the Gospel writer elaborates throughout the book. They are crucial for our understanding of His royal mysteries and His regal mission, signposts that will guide us through turbulent times.

- Read Matthew 4:12–25, and compare Jesus's message with the baptizer's short sermon in 3:2.

We need to establish the chronological context of this scene. The names of the cities unify the three acts. Matthew associates the word *Galilee* with the preaching of Christ (v. 12), the calling of four disciples (v. 18), and the Messiah's ministry of teaching and healing (v. 23). Because John the Gospel writer mentions Jesus's return to the area in John 4:43, the following events in the life of Christ fit chronologically between verses 11 and 12 of Matthew 4, in a period of approximately one year:

- The first meeting with men who would later be called officially to be disciples and specifically apostles (John 1:35–51; see also Luke 6:13)

- The wedding at Cana (John 2:1–12)

- The first cleansing of the temple (John 2:13–25)

- The encounter with Nicodemus (John 3:1–21)

- The conversation with the Samaritan woman (John 4:1–38)

- The negative reaction of the people of Nazareth to Christ's preaching in the local synagogue, which led to His settling in Capernaum (Luke 4:14–30)

Matthew skips these events because he points out that Christ's return to Galilee fulfills the prophecy in Isaiah 9:1–2. He also reveals four realities about Jesus from the official start of His ministry. Assimilating these realities will prepare our hearts to understand His kingdom program.

HIS PRESENCE CONVERTS

When Jesus returned to Galilee, He prefaced His sermons with the announcement, "The time is fulfilled" (Mark 1:15), which associates the official beginning of His ministry with the imprisonment of the forerunner. By linking Jesus's return to the area with fulfillment of prophecy, Matthew demonstrates that even though Christ is the king of the Jews, He is also the Savior of Gentiles, something that becomes clearer throughout the book, but specifically in the end when the risen Christ commissions His disciples to go to the nations (Matthew 28:19–20).

• How does God demonstrate His love to every nation, according to John 3:16?

_____

_____

_____

Jesus demonstrates this love by having an early presence among non-Jews, which would have shocked Matthew's original readers. The former tax collector equates this ministry of presence with the image of light in the background of spiritual darkness, teaching us that Christ converts darkness into light and death into life. Jesus Himself elaborates on the metaphor. According to John 8:12, Christ said, "I am the Light of the world; he who follows Me will not walk in the darkness, but will have the Light of life." He illustrates this truth when after the resurrection He appeared to Saul, the persecutor of the church, who became Paul, the apostle on the road to Damascus. Jesus showed up as light from heaven, so bright that it blinded the man temporarily (Acts 9:3–4).

• How does John use the same image to describe the essence of God, according to 1 John 1:15?

_____

_____

_____

Associations of blessing with light abound in Scripture. For example, God commissioned Israel: "I am the LORD, I have called You in righteousness, I will also hold You by the hand and watch over You, and I will appoint You as a covenant to the people, as a light to the nations, to open blind eyes, to bring out prisoners from the dungeon and those who dwell in darkness from the prison" (Isaiah 42:6–7). The nation failed to fulfill that commission, but Matthew reminds us that the Majestic Savior doesn't fail to bring light to the nations. The picture of Jesus in an area in Israel that became populated by Gentiles demonstrates this truth.

Matthew sets Christ's early Galilean ministry not only in contrast with darkness, but also against the backdrop of "the shadow of death," connecting light and life. More specifically, Jesus brings life, as He clarifies, "I came that they may have life, and have it abundantly" (John 10:10). His presence not only converts darkness into light, but transforms death into life.

Without Christ, people are in complete spiritual darkness, even though they can see the physical world. The shadow of death lurks behind them because even though they exist, they have no spiritual life. Paul helps us understand this when he writes to the Ephesians: "You were dead in your trespasses and sins, in which you formerly walked according to the course of this world, according to the prince of the power of the air, of the spirit that is now working in the sons of disobedience" (Ephesians 2:1–2). The very presence of Jesus distinguishes the life of a believer from an unbeliever. Paul continues: "But God, being rich in mercy, because of His great love with which He loved us, even when we were dead in our transgressions, made us alive together with Christ (by grace you have been saved), and raised us up with Him, and seated us with Him in the heavenly places in Christ Jesus" (Ephesians 2:4–6). If you are in Jesus, you can truly say: "I was sitting in darkness and the shadow of death was upon me, but the light of Christ dawned in my heart. I am truly alive and no longer walk in darkness."

- Read Colossians 1:13, and describe what happened to you when Jesus came into your life.

- Describe one of the ways Jesus draws people to Himself, according to Matthew 5:16.

Tragically, the people of Capernaum rejected that light. Jesus sentences them: "And you, Capernaum, will not be exalted to heaven, will you? You will descend to Hades; for if the miracles had occurred in Sodom which occurred in you, it would have remained to this day" (Matthew 11:23). May this never be said of us.

HIS PREACHING CHALLENGES

After some overlap in the ministries of the forerunner and the King, Jesus picked up where John the Baptist left off, honoring the desire of His cousin: "He must increase, but I must decrease" (John 3:30). Preaching an identical message, Jesus commands repentance and offers the kingdom of heaven to people.

Jesus also equates life with admission to kingdom of heaven. According to Mark 9:45, He instructs His listeners, "If your foot causes you to stumble, cut it off; it is better for you to enter life lame, than, having your two feet, to be cast into hell." Christ uses a figure of speech called *hyperbole* to define character traits of those who enter life (people who deal with their sins properly). Two verses later, using the same literary device, the Majestic Savior links life with the kingdom of God: "If your eye causes you to stumble, throw it out; it is better for you to enter the kingdom of God with one eye, than, having two eyes, to be cast into hell" (Mark 9:47). Therefore, someone who is admitted to the kingdom has received eternal life.

This kingdom was near when John the Baptist announced it but even more so after the forerunner had completed his mission and turned everything over to Christ. Now the King challenges people's misconceptions about becoming a member of His kingdom (and having eternal life) and calls sinners personally to Himself in the process. Shockingly, people then had the impression that they could bypass Jesus to get to heaven on their own merit. Many have the same misconception today as well, probably because they don't like what Jesus said or they associate Him with a set of dos and don'ts.

But His preaching challenges all of that. Elsewhere He says: "No one comes to the Father but through Me" (John 14:6). He offers undeserving sinners a place of honor, a seat at His table in His eternal kingdom. Rather than a set of rules, His invitation displays divine grace in glorious clarity. He calls people to forsake death and embrace life, an opportunity to turn from sin and be made new. The rules of the Christian life are meant to protect us because we are prone to wander, like sheep, and therefore are vulnerable to predators.

Because of the marginal place that the Bible occupies in our culture and Satan's attacks on truth, it is easy to get confused about who Jesus is and what He came here to do. He is not one among equally important religious figures in a spiritual all-you-can-eat buffet. He is not an invention of a group of first-century fishermen. He is not just a rabbi who taught good moral values. He is the Messiah, the King of kings, God's Son, in whom the Father is well-pleased. He came to take the capital punishment you deserve. And He still calls people to Himself today just like He did in the beginning of his Galilean ministry.

HIS PURPOSE CONVINCES

The Sea of Galilee is the Lake of Gennesaret (Luke 5:1), sometimes referred to as the Sea of Tiberias (John 6:1), around which the cities of Capernaum, Bethsaida, and Chorazim were located. Two of the four men fishing already knew something about Jesus. Andrew, for example, had been a disciple of John the Baptist. John describes their first encounter with Christ, approximately a year before:

Again the next day John was standing with two of his disciples, and he looked at Jesus as He walked, and said, "Behold, the Lamb of God!" The two disciples heard him speak, and they followed Jesus. And Jesus turned and saw them following, and said to them, "What do you seek?" They said to Him, "Rabbi (which translated means Teacher), where are You staying?" He said to them, "Come, and you will see." So they came and saw where He was staying; and they stayed with Him that day, for it was about the tenth hour. One of the two who heard John speak and followed Him, was Andrew, Simon Peter's brother. He found first his own brother Simon and said to him, "We have found the Messiah" (which translated means Christ). He brought him to Jesus. Jesus looked at him and said, "You are Simon the son of John; you shall be called Cephas" (which is translated Peter). (John 1:35–42)

Evidently, Peter and Andrew returned to their profession after their initial encounter with Jesus. Possibly the Majestic Savior dismissed them until the proper time when He would call them officially. They didn't hesitate to answer when the time came, because they had been prepared by John the Baptist (and probably were looking forward to the day). Peter, remembering the words of Jesus, "you shall be called a Rock," didn't think twice.

Christ's purpose for their lives, clearly stated, was enough to convince them to leave their profession and their father behind. The many unknown factors in following Jesus could have caused them anxiety, but He attached a promise to the call. He would turn them into evangelists, (Andrew had already brought his brother to Christ) and, later, leaders of the early church. At least one of the four would write New Testament books.

Jesus already called the leaders of the early Christian movement, but He calls every one of His followers to be fishers of men.

- Describe who, how, where, and when you could fish for people who need to hear about Christ, according to the following passages.

Matthew 18:19–20:

Mark 15:16:

Luke 24:46–48:

_____

_____

_____

_____

_____

John 20:21:

_____

_____

_____

_____

Acts 1:8:

_____

_____

_____

_____

_____

You may argue that Jesus directed the Great Commission to that generation of disciples but not to Christians today. Consider that you are a believer today because someone honored this command. That person cared enough about you to lead you to Christ. In fact, since that day two thousand years ago, the church exists because ordinary people turned into fishers of men have been faithful to His disciple-making order. The Great Commission is not the "Awesome Suggestion." Evangelism is not just one of the ministries of the church; it is the reason God hasn't taken us all to heaven yet. He wants us there with Him, but He does not mind waiting—He created time.

HIS PROMINENCE CAPTIVATES

Later in his Gospel, Matthew gives more details of Jesus's sermons. Even though He addressed gentiles, Christ also reached the Jews in the synagogues, Jewish centers of learning that appeared sometime in the period between testaments; they are the predecessors of church buildings.

As a Jew, Jesus would have had access to the local synagogue, just like Paul years later. Christ confirmed the good news of the kingdom with miraculous healings, which accomplished two purposes: (1) to demonstrate His messianic credentials (perfect humanity and absolute divinity united), and (2) to provide a preview of the reality of the kingdom of heaven, where pain, sickness, demonic oppression, and death will be no more. Every time Jesus healed someone, He demonstrated what life in His kingdom will be.

We should not attempt to duplicate these miracles. We're not kings or apostles, the latter of whom had to have seen the risen Jesus to qualify for the ministry. We are witnesses of Christ. Modern-day pastors have no business pretending to perform miraculous healing. If you're sick, you don't have to go to a healing crusade; just call the elders of the church to pray for you (James 5:1). Christ's works authenticated His words. Matthew gives us more detailed accounts of some of those healings throughout the book.

Nothing attracts a crowd more than another crowd. Because of the healings, Christ captivated the multitudes, and His popularity grew. Matthew does not clarify whether everyone who followed Jesus really understood the identity of the Messiah. Perhaps they just wanted a quick fix for their problems. Sadly, many people today will follow Jesus only because they want Him to solve their predicaments, but they abandon Him when they learn of the high cost of discipleship, the call to self-denial. John tells us that many disciples abandoned Him (John 6:66). I hope this does not reflect your level of commitment to Christ.

His presence converts, His preaching challenges, His purpose convinces, and His prominence captivates. These four loadbearing walls support the rest of the Gospel of Matthew. Now that we understand His revered majesty, we are in a good position to embark on a journey through turbulent times to look at twelve specific signposts.

PART TWO
HIS ROYAL MYSTERIES

Signpost 1

God Still Speaks
(MATTHEW 13:1–17)

DAY 1: JESUS INTRODUCES HIS TECHNIQUE (MATTHEW 13:1–9)

God wired the human brain to recognize beauty, art, and craftsmanship in stories. Except angels and people, no one else in the created order appreciates harmony in music, symmetry in sculptures, and depth in paintings. For this reason, His image bearers have been telling and enjoying tales since creation week, passed down through the centuries in written format.

Our generation inherited the art. We admire heroes and despise villains. The plight of protagonists stirs our emotions and arouses our sense of justice. Not surprisingly, Jesus, the Master Storyteller, used this technique often in His teaching. His fictional stories pour the proverbial concrete into abstract ideas and principles. He used this method to illustrate spiritual realities such as heaven and hell and to personify compassion, forgiveness, and faithfulness.

- Read Matthew 25:1–12, and list the principles that the parable of the ten virgins illustrates.

- Read Luke 10:30–37 and list the virtues that the parable of the good Samaritan communicates.

The word *parable* made its way to the English vocabulary from a transliteration of two Greek terms that, when combined, mean "to throw alongside." Parables encourage careful study and stimulate deep reflection.[5] For this reason, Jesus brackets the first cluster of these stories with these verses: "He who has ears, let him hear" (Matthew 13:9) and "Have you understood all these things?" (Matthew 13:51). His teaching in parabolic format transcends time, culture, and even language.

The opening verses in Matthew 13 introduce the parables of the kingdom, known by this description because of the common theme throughout the chapter. See if you can identify a pattern:

"The kingdom of heaven may be compared to a man who sowed good seed in his field" (Matthew 13:24).

"The kingdom of heaven is like a mustard seed" (Matthew 13:31).

"The kingdom of heaven is like leaven" (Matthew 13:33).

"The kingdom of heaven is like a treasure hidden in the field" (Matthew 13:44).

"The kingdom of heaven is like a merchant seeking fine pearls" (Matthew 13:45).

"Again, the kingdom of heaven is like a dragnet cast into the sea, and gathering fish of every kind" (Matthew 13:47).

Jesus tells seven of these immediately after a confrontation with the scribes and Pharisees. He speaks proverbially because He wants to conceal truth from them but reveals mysteries to others.

Let's unpack the first parable.

- Read Matthew 13:1–8, and identify the setting, characters, and plot.

Mark and Luke also record the first parable, which many people know as the parable of the soils, but Christ called it the parable of the sower (see v. 18). The story features elements common to this style of teaching: simplicity, conflict, repetition, mundaneness, and direct application.

Verses 10–17 serve as an interlude between the telling of the parable and its interpretation, but in the opening verses Jesus focuses on the destiny of the metaphorical seeds.

Let's analyze them.

---

5. Leland Ryken, *Words of Delight: A Literary Introduction to the Bible* (Grand Rapids, MI: Baker, 1992), 406.

Scattered Seeds

Jesus's audience, an agrarian society, would have immediately envisioned a farmer casting seeds. They would have also associated the sowing of seeds with gospel proclamation.

Even before we read the explanation of the parable, in verses 18–23, we already have a firm grasp on a spiritual reality: the message of the kingdom is meant to be broadcast, not kept. In other words, people need to hear that God still admits sinners into His kingdom.

- Read Romans 10:14, and answer the three questions in the verse, based on the spiritual reality above.

If you belong to the kingdom of heaven, you are in the business of casting this proverbial seed.

Stolen Seeds

The fictitious farmer does not rely on heavy machinery but walks along the field and sows manually. Naturally, some seed falls by the edge of the field (or the wind blows them) on the unplowed path, impossible to penetrate. As a result, the seeds remain exposed to the birds.

Again, before studying the interpretation from Christ, in the immediate context we can already identify some metaphorical impenetrable hard soils. Because according to the previous chapter, some religious leaders accused Jesus of operating by satanic power, a second spiritual truth emerges: not everyone who hears the gospel embraces it.

Understanding this reality prevents disappointment and frustration in ministry. Overwhelming response to gospel proclamation is the exception—revivals are rare.

Scorched Seeds

Some of the symbolic seeds land on rocky ground, which contains only a shallow layer of fertile soil. From the perspective of the farmer, the field looks ready to produce crops. However, because of the limestone layer underneath (common in ancient Israel), the roots can't reach the nutrients necessary for development. As a result, the sun destroys the little growth that happens.

Once again, the context of the book allows us to unearth another hidden spiritual reality even before looking at the interpretation: superficial association with the gospel message will not endure.

Suffocated Seeds

As carefully as the farmer plows his field, thorns and thistles still manage to take root (perhaps in the corners) and consume resources that the metaphorical seeds need to develop. Scripture gives us an image of conflict and loss.

Sprouted Seeds

The fictitious story breaks the sequence now. This time the proverbial seed lands on soil properly plowed, free from a hidden layer of rocks and weeds. As a result, they grow firmly rooted, produce fruit, and multiply.

The sudden change in pattern yields another spiritual reality about the kingdom of heaven: even though most people who hear the gospel reject it, the ones who respond in faith perpetuate kingdom growth and become sowers themselves.

Jesus encourages careful reflection of this analogy, which illustrates timeless truths. Let's do that.

- Look at the following verses, and identify truths related to casting seeds.

    Matthew 10:7:

    Matthew 13:19:

    Matthew 28:18–20:

- According to Matthew 17:5, how does God still speak today?

DAY 2: JESUS EXPLAINS HIS TECHNIQUE (MATTHEW 13:10–17)

Even though it was common for Jewish teachers of that time to teach in parables, the disciples expressed confusion about Christ's purpose. Did He not want people to hear about the kingdom of heaven?

In His infinite wisdom, Jesus concealed these spiritual realities from a group of people who rejected Him despite the overwhelming evidence of His divinity. The Scribes and Pharisees not only accused Him of operating by the power of Satan (Matthew 12:22–24), but also demanded a sign before they would accept Him as the Messiah.

- Read Matthew 12:38–39, and list the reasons you think the scribes and Pharisees desired a sign from Jesus.

But to another group (people who responded to Him appropriately, His spiritual family who pursue the will of the Father; see 12:49–50), He revealed realities of His kingdom.

In biblical language, a mystery is not an enigma, but something only partially revealed and not fully understood. In verse 11, Jesus uses this description to refer to God's redemptive plan and remind the disciples about His sovereignty. God granted them access to the truth.

- According to John 8:32, what happens when a sinner learns the truth about Christ and embraces it? When did that happen to you? Who shared the truth with you?

Although the Jews expected the messianic kingdom, they rejected Christ when He showed up as a Suffering Servant rather than a Conquering General. The King would be killed, rise from the dead, ascend back to heaven, and postpone His earthly rule "until the fullness of Gentiles has come in" (Romans 11:25). That's one of the mysteries of the kingdom.

But you ask, "If Jesus is King, why isn't He ruling now?"

We live in the time when the King of kings rules from heaven. In the meantime, He commands members of His kingdom to sow the seeds of the gospel while the Holy Spirit, who indwells believers, equips us for the task. One day He will gather His harvest into His barn, an image from another kingdom parable.

- Read Romans 16:25–26, and summarize the way Paul associates the gospel with a mystery previously concealed.

_____

_____

_____

- Read Colossians 1:26–27, and identify the mystery Paul describes. According to this passage, where else does King Jesus reign from?

_____

_____

_____

Amazingly, Jesus switches methodologies and teaches His disciples in non-parabolic format (see v. 14). He reveals to them that they just witnessed fulfillment of prophecy (Isaiah 6:9–10). The scribes and Pharisees could not appreciate (or even grasp) biblical truth and therefore, epitomized the ultimate tragedy: to come so close to the pearls and behave like pigs, a metaphor from Matthew 7:6.

In contrast, if you belong to the kingdom of heaven, God already pronounced you supremely fortunate, immeasurably happy, and indescribably favored, because you have access to the mysteries of the kingdom, according to verse 16.

For this reason, every time we grumble about life circumstances, health, finances, family, job, or church, we disagree with God. When we complain that we are not blessed enough, we might as well tell Him, "My definition of blessedness is more accurate than yours. You say I am blessed because I am in Christ, and I say that's not enough. I need another spouse, another job, the loaded bank account, and so on, to be truly blessed." Can you think of anything more blasphemous?

- Read Matthew 12:31, and list forgivable sins and the unforgivable sin.

_____

_____

_____

- Read Romans 8:1, and answer the question, "Could I ever commit the unpardonable sin?"

- Read Romans 8:38–39, and fill in the blank. "I will never lose my salvation because _____."

I invite you to look at your life from the perspective stated in verse 16. Just like that first generation of disciples, you understand divine revelation now only because God has opened your spiritual eyes and ears. You enjoy unimaginable blessedness not because of your noble quest for truth, but because such a position is a gift from an infinitely kind God.

- Read Matthew 5:3–12, and itemize your blessings.

Do you realize how blessed you are? We have nothing to fear. God loves you so much that He has revealed to you how to get into His kingdom. If you responded to the message, "by His doing you are in Christ Jesus" (1 Corinthians 1:30). Never take that for granted. Share this message with someone who does not enjoy this state of indescribable blessedness.

SIGNPOST 2

GOD STILL SAVES
(MATTHEW 13:18–19A)

DAY 1: THE ANNOUNCERS AND THE ANNOUNCEMENT (MATTHEW 13:18)

In his book titled *Words of Delight*, author Leland Ryken points out that the simplicity of the parable of the sower arouses our interest in what's below the surface (no pun intended).[6] He is right; the story makes us want to read more to discover the hidden treasures. Because God knows how easily we can misinterpret parables, He preserved the interpretation from Christ in written form through the centuries.

In the preview chapter, we concluded that God still speaks. In this lesson, we will verify that He still saves.

- Read Matthew 13:18–19a, and summarize the message that the metaphorical seed illustrates.

Jesus offered the kingdom of heaven to Israel first, but the Jews of the time declined the offer. His followers might have wondered, "What's going to happen now that Jews failed to acknowledge the King and His kingdom? Has God rejected Israel?"

Because His own people refused to acknowledge Him, Christ postponed the establishment of His millennial kingdom. During that time, God will fulfill every promise He made to the nation. Before Jesus establishes a theocracy on earth, upon His return, Israel will finally recognize Him as the Jewish Messiah. In the meantime, people from every tribe and tongue who respond to the gospel populate the heavenly kingdom (and will return with Him). Jesus elaborates by telling His Jewish listeners, "Behold, your house is being left to you desolate! For I say to you, from now on you will not see Me until you say, 'BLESSED IS HE WHO COMES IN THE NAME OF THE LORD!'" (Matthew 23:39).

---

6. Ryken, *Words of Delight*, 410. Parenthesis mine.

In the parable of the sower, He reveals details about the time between His first and second coming—our time, when the King rules from His throne in heaven and at the same time lives in the hearts of believers, something only partially revealed in the Old Testament—the mystery form of His kingdom.

Here's the first feature of this royal mystery.

Jesus does not identify the announcers, but we can deduce their identity from other parts of Scripture. For example, John the Baptist and Jesus form the first group; the first serves as the forerunner of the latter.

- How did John prepare the way for Christ according to the passages below?

    Malachi 3:1:

    _____

    _____

    _____

    Isaiah 40:3:

    _____

    _____

    _____

    John 1:19–23:

    _____

    _____

    _____

John himself clarified the temporary nature of his ministry when he affirmed, "He must increase, but I must decrease" (John 3:30). His prophetic ministry of announcing the King and the kingdom led to his arrest and martyrdom, but as soon as the forerunner was incarcerated, Jesus picked up where John left off. (See Matthew 4:17.)

The first disciples constitute the second group of kingdom announcers. Jesus sent them to the lost sheep of Israel (Matthew 10:6), but by the end of the Gospel of Matthew, Christ commissioned them to go to all the nations (Matthew 28:19). Before His ascension, He reminded them to witness even in the most remote part of the world (Acts 1:8).

- Read Peter's sermon at Pentecost, from Acts 2:14–36, and outline the main points. What nations (ethnicities) did he reach? Hint: read Acts 2:5–13.

- Read Stephen's speech in Acts 7:2–53, and outline the main points. Compare the immediate response of his audience with Peter's audience from the text above.

Church-age saints get to proclaim the kingdom today and form the third group of announcers. Because taking the gospel to every nation and ethnicity would be impossible for the eleven disciples, the second generation of Christ followers and future generations after them would perpetuate the process. For this reason, every Christian since then must embrace the call to make disciples.

- Read Acts 8:4–40, and describe how the gospel spread to other ethnicities.

- Read Acts 13 through 15, and trace Paul's first missionary journey. Note people's response to the message. How are they similar to or different from how people respond today?

- Read Luke 24:46–47 and John 20:21, and write your responsibility as a modern-day believer. List your fears and hesitations.

Consider this: You will not serve God at full potential until you start sharing Christ with unbelievers. You are also missing out on the highest honor God can ever give you in this life. Like John the Baptist, you have a limited opportunity to preach Jesus; there will be no evangelism in heaven. One day, God will rapture the church, at which point He will raise the fourth group of kingdom announcers.

Tribulation saints will become Christians after that day and will sow seeds of the kingdom during the seven years that precede the return of Christ. One hundred forty-four thousand Jews (twelve thousand from each tribe of Israel) will join them.

• Read Revelation 7:4–8, and list the heads of the tribes by name.

• Read Revelation 7:14 and 14:1–5, and describe the ministry and calling of the Tribulation martyrs.

• Read Revelation 11:3–4, and list other notable announcers in the tribulation of the end times and their peculiarities. Could they be the people from the Old Testament who never experienced physical death? If so, who are they?

After encouraging his disciples to assimilate the truth in the parable, Jesus calls their attention to the second feature of the kingdom of heaven in mystery form.

Christ identifies the proverbial seed as "the word of the kingdom." John the Baptist started broadcasting, "Repent, for the kingdom of heaven is at hand" (Matthew 3:2), but when the forerunner concluded his ministry, Jesus preached the same message and, after teaching His disciples these royal mysteries, He instructed them to "preach, saying, 'The kingdom of heaven is at hand'" (10:7).

Do you see the pattern? Christ expects modern-day disciples to repeat the announcement. We are stewards, not the originators, of the message. We don't have His permission to modify the seed in order to accommodate the different soils.

But what if people don't want to hear?

You will never know until you ask. People decline or receive the message conditionally because of the state of their hearts (illustrated by the types of soils). Unless God opens their eyes, the gospel makes no sense to them, regardless of its simplicity. They consider the message of the kingdom foolishness—not sophisticated enough, not enlightening enough, not people-centered enough.

- Read 1 Corinthians 1:23–24, and describe the message Paul and the other apostles preached. According to this message, how does someone enter the kingdom of heaven?

- How does Jesus's symbolic language in Matthew 7:13 relate to the above passage?

Casting the seed of the message of the kingdom always invites opposition, which leads us to the third reality of the kingdom in mystery form.

DAY 2: THE ANTAGONIST AND THE AUDIENCE (MATTHEW 13:19A)

Jesus identifies the antagonist by his title: Satan is the evil one who snatches the seed from the soil.

- Read Isaiah 14:13–14, and describe how the "I will" statements reveal the devil's desire to steal the gospel message from people's hearts.

The devil blinds the minds of unbelievers (2 Corinthians 4:4) and promotes counterfeit religions. A liar and a murderer from the beginning (John 8:44), he entices the lust of the flesh and eyes and the pride of life (1 John 2:16). He accomplishes his purposes by deceiving the nations (Revelation 20:3) and by slandering and assaulting the character of believers to discredit the message we preach.

Satan has been extremely successful in our corner of the world. We don't think of Western society as primitive because few people worship graven images in our culture. But most of us burn incense to our own accomplishments and desires. We offer our devotion not to idols of wood or stone, but to self-fulfillment. Worshipers who gather at the altar of human achievement find nothing appealing about a narrow gate to heaven, a message of self-denial, self-sacrifice, and humans' inability to earn salvation. The evil one knows this well. He has observed human nature for millennia.

- According to Ephesians 6:11, how do we neutralize the schemes of the devil?

- Read Ephesians 6:13–17, and list each component of the metaphorical protective covering.

Because Satan likes to slander believers, I want you to imagine the following scene: The devil approaches the divine throne (Scripture says he has access to God; see Job 2:1) and says, "You gotta be kidding. You have Pierre in Oregon preaching your Word and shepherding your people. I can't think of anyone more incompetent. The guy comes from a broken home. What does he know about family life and godly marriage? His father, an eloquent atheist, was on my team."

Or he may say this about you: "God, really? You're going to use him, the former drug addict and adulterer, to sow gospel seed? And what about her, the former fornicator? Remember her abortion? They used to serve me very effectively, I might add. What a pathetic team you have."

Then God calls Christ to the scene and says, "Let's hear from their advocate, my Son, the righteous [1 John 2:1] in whom I am well pleased."

Then Jesus takes the stand and says, "They are the elect of God [Romans 8:33], the blessed of My Father [Matthew 5:3-11], the people for My own possession [Titus 2:14], living stones built up for a holy priesthood [1 Peter 2:5], and the sheep of My Father's pasture [Psalm 79:13]. My Father gave them to me [John 10:29]. I will never leave them orphans [John 14:18]. No one will snatch them out of my hand [John 10:28]. Nothing will ever separate them from my love [Romans 8:35]. They are more than conquerors [Romans 8:37]. They follow me, and I will make them fishers of men [Matthew 4:19]. I am coming quickly, and I am ready to reward them" [Revelation 22:12].

He rests His case.

The accuser of the brethren may want to undo your sowing by discrediting and discouraging you, but the Father has justified you. You are free to continue to sow the Word of the kingdom. Don't let anything or anyone stop that.

The fourth reality of the kingdom emerges in Jesus's explanation of the parable of the sower: Faithful sowers have taken the good news to this global audience since the day of Christ's ascension. Casting the seeds of the gospel may be hard work, but it is a simple activity. You don't need a seminary degree to lead people to Christ; it takes commitment and compassion. Just like a sower labors in the field, rain or sunshine, flocks of birds hovering above or not, you just need to get to work. Consider this, The Lord of the harvest does not recruit clever, larger-than-life, celebrity sowers—only faithful ones.

We must broadcast the word of the kingdom until God calls us home. We don't know where the metaphorical seed will land, but cast we must. I don't know about you, but I long to hear, "Well done, good and faithful slave . . . enter into the joy of your master" (Matthew 25:21).

When I share the gospel, I am aware that some people, even fellow sowers, will oppose and reject me, but I know that the Holy Spirit works both as a plow and a scarecrow to allow seed to penetrate the good soil. God has granted my request for fruit many times, including some of my family members. I pray for Him to give me endurance even when I can't see an immediate crop. I pray the same for you.

- List names of people with whom you will share the gospel this week.

SIGNPOST 3

GOD STILL SURPRISES
(MATTHEW 13:19B–23)

DAY 1: TOTAL REJECTION AND TEMPORARY DEVOTION (MATTHEW 13:19–21)

Let's get situated contextually again. By chapter 12 of Matthew's Gospel, the Pharisees' unwillingness to acknowledge Christ as the Messiah had turned into hostility. They rejected His works and His words but could not ignore His miracles, so they attributed His power to Satan. Jesus warns that this type of unbelief leads to eternal condemnation. The religious elite of Israel of that time also demanded a sign from Him, but Jesus did not cater to their sinful demands.

The reaction of the Pharisees surprised the disciples, which prompted Christ to clarify that in the mystery form of the kingdom not everybody would respond equally to the gospel. According to Him, the different types of soil correspond to the conditions of people's hearts when exposed to the good news.

Here is the first type of response to the King in the mystery form of the kingdom.

The proverbial seed does not penetrate because the soil has hardened. Blinded by their religiosity and self-righteousness, the scribes and Pharisees refused to admit their need for grace. Tax collectors and prostitutes may have been outside of God's favor, but not them, according to their belief system. For that reason, they rejected a nonpolitical Messiah.

The scenario happens often today. Sin hardens the hearts of people so much that the gospel cannot penetrate the outer layer unless God intervenes. People may be hardened by pride, like the Pharisees and scribes, or they may believe they stand beyond salvation. Both extremes tend to produce unbelief because they allow Satan the opportunity to snatch gospel seeds.

- Read Matthew 13:25, and identify the other farming imagery Jesus uses to illustrate Satan's opposition.

The devil works around the clock sabotaging our sowing. He replaces the Word of the kingdom with other seeds; churches that are not gospel centered make his job easier. Can you think of a more urgent time than now to refocus on the death, burial, and resurrection of Christ?

We don't primarily invite people to join our church (something of secondary importance). We don't ask people to change teams (i.e., join a denomination). We inform them how to be admitted into the kingdom of heaven, by grace through faith in Christ alone. That is the good seed.

How should we deal with hardened hearts? We lament when people reject Jesus; we may even shed tears of compassion. We must beg God for their lives and ask for the Holy Spirit to till the ground. But rejection should not stop us. We will eventually encounter receptive hearts, soil prepared by God.

- Read Paul's testimony in Galatians 1:13–17, and describe how the seed destined for the belly of a metaphorical bird penetrated this initially bad soil. Did you reject the gospel the first time you heard it?

Similar transformations happen every day. The problem for Satan is that the Holy Spirit is also in the farming business. He plows the ground in people's hearts and prepares them to receive the King. The devil blinds the eyes of unbelievers, but Jesus gives sight to the blind.

You embraced Christ because the Holy Spirit worked in your heart beforehand. The credit belongs to Christ alone.

- Read Romans 1:18. How did you suppress the truth before your conversion?

Notice that the second analogy presents a ground soft enough for the seed to penetrate, but the roots can't reach the nutrients needed for development because of the rocky layer in the soil. As a result, the seed shoots up only to be scorched by the sun. The sower gets the initial impression of immediate results and might even be tempted to dedicate more time to this apparently fruitful crop, but the superficiality becomes evident by how the crop responds to the heat.

According to Jesus, some people demonstrate initial interest in Him. They seem to embrace the gospel at first, but their enthusiasm lasts only until the first trial. (By the way, notice that the heat from affliction affects every seed.)

The natural process of maturity includes affliction. We live in a fallen world, yet to be restored. Faith not rooted firmly in the Word of God will succumb to tribulation.

The people who Jesus describes in verses 20–21 usually select the elements of the gospel that suit their felt needs, perhaps the less confrontational aspects of the message. They show up periodically because of a favorite teacher, a preferred style of worship, a particular cause, a friend, the chance to meet a potential spouse, but usually they show little desire to serve others. They quit as soon as they realize Christianity is not about them. I am afraid they have counterfeit faith, clearly identified by shallowness.

False believers have no reason to endure hardship. Why suffer criticism, rejection, and ridicule if they only embraced Jesus to get through a season? How do we interact with these superficial responses? We can't see the root, but we can observe their fruit.

- Read Luke 15:1–11, and identify the other figure of speech used by Jesus (notice the agriculture motif) and His commands and promises.

DAY 2: TRAGIC DECEPTION AND TRUE SALVATION (MATTHEW 13:22–23)

Similar to the previous type of response, the next group of people's identification with Christ only lasts until God puts their faith through a different kind of test. In the previous category, affliction and persecution reveal the counterfeit nature of some responses to the gospel. In this example the tests are affluence and preoccupation. One usually leads to the other.

The wealthier you are, the greater your temptation to worry about maintaining your status. (There is nothing wrong with having money, but you don't want money to have you.) Jesus warned His followers constantly against trusting riches, the love of which is the root of all evil and keeps people from receiving the gospel.

Here's how the worry of the world and the deceitfulness of wealth can strangle the seed of the gospel sown in people's hearts: if you live in the United States, you belong to one of the wealthiest societies in the world. But while our nation may be rich materially, we are also one of the neediest mission fields. Americans have embraced the deceitfulness of wealth, evident by our hunger for consumption. We have an insatiable appetite for more stuff, simply for the sake of consuming. Sadly, we bring that behavior to our churches and act like customers rather than servants, an audience rather than a flock.

Clever advertisers have taught us to associate self-worth with the ability to impress by what we own. Why do you think people camp in front of a store three days before the launch of a smartphone that costs $1,000 when a similar phone sells for $99 in the mall down the street? Or why would you buy a $700 pair of designer shoes on credit when a less glamorous (and more comfortable) one sells for $30? We make irrational purchase decisions because we want to appear successful and more attractive. We want people to pay attention to us because of a God-given desire to be loved gone wrong.

But "God demonstrates His own love toward us, in that while we were yet sinners, Christ died for us" (Romans 5:8). The love people are willing to sacrifice for does not cost anything; it is a free gift of God.

- Read John 3:16, and identify the way in which God has loved you.

Many people reject Christ because in their minds, identification with Jesus threatens their perception of success and sophistication. Case in point: the scribes and Pharisees of Jesus's day. They would have objected that Jesus could not be the King because kings are born is palaces, not in mangers. The deceitfulness of wealth and the worry of the world caused them to miss the kingdom of heaven.

How should we interact with people strangled by wealth and worry? According to Paul, we must reason with them not "to fix their hope on the uncertainty of riches, but on God, who richly supplies us with all things to enjoy" (1 Timothy 6:17).

- Read 1 Timothy 6:18–19, and identify the virtues Paul instructs his young friend to teach.

- Read Philippians 4:12–13, and articulate the biblical perspective on dealing with prosperity and adversity.

Jesus compares people who hear and understand the message with the good soil. This does not mean God grants salvation to people who are good by nature. If this were the case, we would all be doomed, because "all have sinned and fall short of the glory of God" (Romans 3:23).

In this parable, the good soil symbolizes a receptive heart, one that the Holy Spirit has prepared. According to Christ, the Third Person of the Trinity "will convict the world concerning sin and righteousness and judgment" (John 16:8). Speaking of good soil, did you notice that saved people always produce fruit, some more than others?

- Read Psalm 1:1–3, and identify the connection between the good soil and a healthy tree.

- Read Matthew 28:19–20, and describe the process of reproduction in disciple-making.

Notice the contrast between the fruitful crop (v. 8) and the sprout scorched by the heat of affliction and persecution (v. 5). Genuine salvation not only produces fruit, it endures everything. True believers persevere even though we may fall into sin occasionally. We get up again, not because of our ability, but because of the One who equips us to press on. Why else would Paul tell Timothy, "Suffer hardship with me, as a good soldier of Christ Jesus" (2 Timothy 2:3)?

Consider your present adversity a season of growth and fruit-bearing, an opportunity for Christ to be glorified in you more remarkably so that your confidence in Him will grow to the next level.

Speaking of faith that endures hardship, here's the last lesson in the parable: according to Jesus, more people reject than respond in true faith when exposed to the gospel. Knowing this keeps sowers from having unbiblical expectations and prevents pastors from discouragement, burnout, or being run out of churches.

Sowers are not responsible for people's responses. We will only fail if we don't sow the seeds of the gospel. We will betray Him if we tamper with the seed to suit the tastes of sinners. What's the faithful alternative? We must sow continually.

Spiritually speaking, the church is in the agricultural business. This metaphor embarrasses some believers because they prefer to pursue the more popular self-improvement approach; motivational speakers get more followers. But if we want to be faithful, we sow seeds, harvest fruit, recruit more sowers, and perpetuate the process. The Perfect Farmer gives the growth in His time and season. When we get weary, we build each other up, encourage one another, and return to the field.

I am recruiting you today for Seed Sowing 101. Keep in mind many people will reject your message. These rejections will frustrate you, but you can rejoice over the ones who embrace the gospel and bear fruit.

How can I conclude this chapter without asking, What kind of soil are you? Is your heart so hard the gospel can't penetrate? So cluttered with rocks the message can't develop roots? Is the scorching heat of affliction tempting you to abandon the faith? Is your heart so filled with worry and the pursuit of wealth that the good seed can't breathe? Or is your heart ready to bear fruit?

GOD STILL SUSTAINS
(MATTHEW 13:24-30, 36-43)

DAY 1: SOWING AND SABOTAGING (MATTHEW 13:24-28A)

If you lived in ancient Israel during the time of Jesus and wanted to undercut your competitor, you would sneak into his farm at night and pour salt all over his field. But if you really wanted to devastate the man's livelihood, you would sow tares among wheat in his farm. The next day no one would notice the bad seeds, outwardly identical to the good ones. The roots of the two would intertwine to the point that only a skilled laborer could uproot them properly. Malicious oversowing caused so much devastation to farmers that Rome enacted legislation against it.

The next kingdom parable in Matthew 13 describes this shrewd practice. Because Jesus's audience lived in an agrarian society, they identified the context immediately. He repeats the farming theme from the first parable, but this time adds the stealth of an enemy who attempts to sabotage kingdom work.

Matthew recorded this parable because God wants us to understand another aspect of His redemptive plan, unique to the time of the kingdom in mystery form. We can also call this mystery age (our current time) the period between the rejection of the King and His return.

Let's understand more mysteries of the kingdom of heaven.

The story presents an antagonist who wants to destroy the work of the protagonist. Whereas in the first parable, Jesus focused on the soil, in this one a crafty culprit takes the stage, followed by a wise and patient landowner. The Master Storyteller draws our attention to two types of seed. First, He associates three components with the good seed present in the kingdom during the temporary physical absence of the King (13:24).

1. **The Farmer (Matthew 13:37): "And He said, 'The one who sows the good seed is the Son of Man.'"**

   • According to this verse, who is the protagonist? Hint: see Matthew 8:20; 9:6; and 10:23.

- Read John 18:36, and identify the origin of Christ's kingdom.

Christ both inaugurates the kingdom of heaven and sustains it by overseeing its growth. The Divine King became flesh, dwelt among people, and sowed His kingdom on the earth. His own kin rejected Him, so He postponed the establishment of His earthly rule until the time Israel will acknowledge their Messiah on a national scale.

- Read Romans 11:25–26, and describe the mystery that Paul reveals.

2. **The Field (Matthew 13:38a): "And the field is the world."**

Jesus does not associate the soil with the church in this parable; He would have used the same word He did in Matthew 16:18 to clarify that the gates of hades would not overpower the assembly of His people. However, God does manifest the kingdom of heaven in and through His church.

- Read 1 Corinthians 12:13, and identify where God places new members of His kingdom.

The field also represents the world beyond the borders of Israel, which would have sparked the curiosity (and perhaps frustration) of the disciples; God welcomes gentiles to the kingdom of heaven. Furthermore, Jesus clarifies that even though He refers to His kingdom as a heavenly rule, He plants it in the physical world. In other words, Christ has royal authority in both realms.

- According to the possessive pronoun at the end of Matthew 13:24, who has sole possession of the world?

- Read Revelation 5:9, and describe the One who has the right to rule the universe, according to the heavenly choir.

- According to Colossians 1:16, why does He have property rights to the universe?

- Read Hebrews 1:3, and describe how He sustains the universe.

Did you know you don't really own your house? Neither does the bank that holds your loan. The Father has delegated all authority to His Son, who declares, "All authority has been given to Me in heaven and on earth" (Matthew 28:18). Therefore, Jesus has complete jurisdiction to build His kingdom in the world.

Satan may be "the god of this world" (2 Corinthians 4:4) and "the prince of the power of the air" (Ephesians 2:2), but there has never been (and there will never be) a change of ownership. The devil and his hosts have temporary and limited access to Christ's field.

3. **The Family (Matthew 13:38b): "and as for the good seed, these are the sons of the kingdom."**

Contrary to the first parable, the seed in this one illustrates not a message, but people. Because all have sinned and fall short of the glory of God (Romans 3:23), Jesus qualifies this illustration in terms of divinely imputed favor upon believers. The sons of the kingdom are "good" only because we receive Christ's righteousness at the moment of salvation. And no seed can self-plant, which means that unless Jesus redeems sinners, no one can enter His kingdom. Thankfully, He welcomes whoever believes in Him (John 3:16) and addresses members with terms that remind us of our adoption.

- Read 2 Corinthians 6:18; 1 John 3:1; and Romans 8:1; and identify your status as a member of God's kingdom.

- According to 1 Corinthians 1:30 and 1 Peter 1:3, who admitted you into the kingdom of heaven?

Jesus could have called us slaves of the King, subjects of His kingdom, or servants of His realm—and He would be accurate)—but in this parable He calls us "sons," a term that communicates His everlasting affection for His people.

4. **The Fraud (Matthew 13:38c): "And the tares are the sons of the evil one."**

The bad seed represents opposition to kingdom work. Jesus shows His listeners the picture of counterfeit sons, attached to and indistinguishable from genuine believers. The tares symbolize children of Satan, planted in the kingdom to cause damage.

- Read Matthew 3:7, and identify sons of the evil one posing as sons of the kingdom.

The Pharisees wanted everyone to see them as genuine sons of the kingdom, but they didn't realize Satan sowed them in order to deceive people. However, this revealed mystery does not give us permission to label our critics or persecutors as diabolical implants. Until they reach a certain level of development, we can't differentiate wheat from tare. Spiritually, we are not skilled reapers.

Often, people who act like bad seed turn out to be strong-willed sheep that bite their shepherds occasionally. They are genuine believers who don't need to be uprooted, but shepherded lovingly, graciously, and patiently toward repentance. If they insist on their sinful behavior, we should activate church discipline, but we must not succumb to the temptation to call someone a fraud prematurely. We can't see the root, so we must suspend judgment until we can see the fruit.

- Read Matthew 18:15–18, and identify the steps of church discipline.

5. **The Foe (Matthew 13:39): "and the enemy who sowed them is the devil."**

The parable of the tares reveals one of Satan's strategies during the mystery form of the kingdom of heaven; he infiltrates bad seeds in the world. Every false religion that ever existed, including pseudo-Christian systems (aka cults) and even atheism (which I call the worship of foolishness because the fool says in his heart "there is no God," according to Psalm 14:1), originated in the mind of the evil one.

While Satan has limited autonomy to sabotage kingdom work in the world, he prefers to infiltrate the church. Because he has achieved tremendous success, he wants to perfect the strategy. Why would he focus his efforts anywhere else? The devil already harvests his malevolent fruit daily in government agencies and the entertainment industry, for example.

Professing believers sometimes act like practical unbelievers because Satan sows bad seed in the world, especially in the church. According to Jesus, sons of the devil mingle with the sons of the kingdom so well that we can't tell them apart until they expose their nature.

During this time of coexistence between good and bad seed, we must preserve the purity of the church by confronting sin and exercising church discipline, confident that Christ maintains total control of the growth of His kingdom.

- According to Revelation 20:1–2, what will happen to Satan in the millennial kingdom? Will he be able to sow anything?

- Read Revelation 20:7–10, and identify Satan's destination.

According to this parable, the tares eventually reveal themselves. The concerned workers want to neutralize the satanic sabotage, which leads us to the second part of this royal mystery.

DAY 2: BUNDLING AND BURNING (MATTHEW 13:28–30)

Understandably, the fictitious workers wanted to purge the field. They volunteered to avenge the master and undo the work of the enemy. They wanted to see the tares burn, a picture of future judgment. But because of their limited knowledge, they offered a less-than-perfect plan.

The Problematic Solution (13:28b)

The workers were not equipped for the purging. They may have accidentally hurt the sons of the kingdom in the process because the roots of the wheat and tares grew interwoven. Only a skilled harvester could untangle the two.

The immediate context clarifies that the workers symbolize the disciples listening to the explanation. They longed to see the kingdom of heaven in all its purity and glory. They also wanted to see the sons of the evil one blasted out of existence.

- Read Acts 1:6, and describe the messianic expectation of the disciples.

Particularly, James and John reflected this sentiment when they asked Jesus, after witnessing people reject Him, "Lord, do You want us to command fire to come down from heaven and consume them?" (Luke 9:54). But Christ rebuked them: "The Son of Man did not come to destroy men's lives, but to save them" (Luke 9:56). Judgment would happen later.

Who among us doesn't share the disciples' desire to see a purging of the world? Unbelievers do what they do because, by divine permission, Satan planted them alongside the sons of the kingdom. They work at the same places we do. We attend the same schools. Some of you share a house with them. But we desire their salvation, not their condemnation.

God will allow them to develop until He says, "Time's up." His patience will eventually run out. In the meantime, He has not called us to uproot the sons of the evil one; we will cause damage if we attempt to do it. Only God judges righteously (1 Peter 2:23), because only He knows true motivation.

According to Matthew 7:16, believers should inspect the fruit (what we can see), not the root (what we cannot see) of suspected bad seed. We leave the bundling and burning to the Lord.

He offers a better option than the problematic solution for dealing with the sons of the evil one.

The Proper Strategy

According to Jesus, God's plan for cleaning His field (the purification of His kingdom) has four elements.

1. **The Consummation (Matthew 13:39b): "And the harvest is the end of the age."**

Divine judgment will happen at the end times. Meanwhile, sons of the kingdom must confront evil by calling on people to repent and come to Christ.

We want people to be bundled, not burned. We were once sons of disobedience (Ephesians 2:2), but we received salvation, not condemnation.

- Read Romans 8:1, and identify one the greatest blessings of being in God's kingdom.

2. **The Collaboration (Matthew 13:39c): "And the reapers are angels."**

The appointed harvesters will execute judgment. In the meantime, sons of the kingdom must fulfill their duty as proclaimers of good news. Many believers hurt their brothers and sisters because they misunderstand their role in the kingdom.

- Read Galatians 6:1, and identify the believer's duty toward a believer caught in sin.

We must warn people to flee the wrath to come, but we only ignite the flames of revival, not the fires of inquisition. According to the first parable, God commissioned angels to bundle some and burn others at the appropriate time.

3. **The Condemnation (Matthew 13:40–42): "So just as the tares are gathered up and burned with fire, so shall it be at the end of the age. The Son of Man will send forth His angels, and they will gather out of His kingdom all stumbling blocks, and those**

who commit lawlessness, and will throw them into the furnace of fire; in that place there will be weeping and gnashing of teeth."

The furnace symbolizes the lake of fire in Revelation 19:20, a reference to the tragic end of everyone who refuses to come to Christ. The harvesting angels will remove Satan's bad seed from the world. In the meantime, sons of the kingdom should notify the bad seeds that God can transform them into good seeds.

We live in the age of grace. Clearly but kindly, God draws people to Himself, inviting them to repent. He promises to be merciful to our iniquities and remember our sins no more (Hebrews 8:12).

- Read Isaiah 1:18, and identify God's promise of restoration.

- According to Isaiah 43:25, how does God deal with forgiven sins of His people?

- According to Acts 3:19, what does God recommend for sinners in order to have sins wiped away?

- Read the following Bible verses and list any attributes of God you see.

  Micah 7:18–19:

Daniel 9:9:

_____

_____

_____

_____

Like Paul, we reason with sinners: "We beg you on behalf of Christ, be reconciled to God" (2 Corinthians 5:20). Here's what awaits those who have been reconciled to him:

4. **The Conclusion (Matthew 13:43b): "Then THE RIGHTEOUS WILL SHINE FORTH AS THE SUN in the kingdom of their Father. He who has ears, let him hear."**

The people who God declares righteous have the opposite destination at the harvest. Sons will shine forth because the Shekinah glory of God will replace the light from the biggest star in our solar system. The New Jerusalem, the capital city of our Father's kingdom, "has no need of the sun or of the moon to shine on it, for the glory of God has illumined it, and its lamp is the Lamb" (Revelation 21:23).

You just learned another mystery of the kingdom of heaven: Sowing and sabotaging now, bundling and burning in the future. Let me suggest one point of reflection.

The evil that you see in the world today is only there by divine permission to fulfill God's sovereign purposes. One day, the government will rest on His shoulders (Isaiah 9:6), and the King of kings will make a new heaven and a new world (Revelation 21:1). Make sure you secure a place in His barn.

SIGNPOST 5

GOD STILL SUCCEEDS
(MATTHEW 13:31–33)

DAY 1: REGIONAL INAUGURATION FOLLOWED BY UNIVERSAL INFLUENCE (MATTHEW 13:31-32)

The Tohoku tsunami of 2011 off the coast of Japan originated from an earthquake on the ocean floor, thirty-seven miles offshore. The seismic activity produced relatively small waves in the epicenter, but the ripples soon turned into 130-foot monstrosities that reached as far as six miles inland, wiping out everything in their path.

This natural phenomenon illustrates the royal mystery Jesus reveals in the next two parables in Matthew 13. His critics would have complained, "I don't see the kingdom this man claims to bring. He doesn't wear a royal robe, doesn't sit on a throne, and does not carry a scepter. Where is the glamour? Where are His armies, castle, and imperial court?"

They had these responses in part because transfer of power at that time happened either by dynastic succession, coup, or revolution. The Jews expected the Messiah to establish His kingdom by crushing their gentile oppressors.

But on another occasion Jesus clarified, "My kingdom is not of this world. If My kingdom were of this world, then My servants would be fighting so that I would not be handed over to the Jews; but as it is, My kingdom is not of this realm" (John 18:36). He speaks of the heavenly origin of His rule. In fact, His domain defies every human expectation. First, the King of kings was born in a manger, not in a palace. He grew up in obscurity, learning an ordinary profession until His forerunner announced the arrival of the Messiah, at which point Christ recruited not warriors, but fishermen and even a tax collector. He befriended sinners and demonstrated compassion to gentiles. Jesus's critics couldn't see how this Man qualified as a King.

The disciples might have associated the Jews' rejection of Christ with failure. To clarify that nothing could be further from the truth, Jesus speaks in parabolic form of a fascinating aspect of His kingdom: an unimpressive beginning that grows into worldwide dominion.

If the first parable pictures the proclamation of the kingdom and the second speaks of opposition to the kingdom, the next two emphasize the expansion of the kingdom.

If we misunderstand this feature of God's program, we will think the unfolding of His redemptive plan depends on human effort, like a corporation that must develop a creative marketing strategy if it intends to survive ever-changing cultural trends. The kingdom of heaven does not operate like that. God will spread its reach despite opposition, persecution, or secularization (the "de-Christianization" of the West) regardless of who serves as president, king, czar, emperor, or pope.

In fact, human government plays no role in, and doesn't interfere with, the expansion of the kingdom of heaven, which will continue to penetrate the world as faithful believers proclaim the gospel boldly, lovingly, and clearly, whether we do it under representative republics, communist regimes, socialist systems, or absolute monarchies.

Subjects of the kingdom of heaven belong to the only unstoppable institution that will sweep the entire universe one day. Opposition may stop individual believers temporarily, but God will always equip His people to do His work, according to the lesson in the next two parables of the kingdom.

The first of the two parallel parables retains the agriculture motif. As He did in the previous two, Jesus pictures a farmer sowing in a field. Because of His disclaimer in verse 13, His listeners may not have understood the divine artistry and the disciples may not have grasped the lesson immediately.

Before we move further, let's address the biblical inerrancy question. Bible critics often take issue with this parable. They point out that the mustard seed is not the smallest in the world. I offer two responses.

First, Christ's lips can never utter a lie because He is the truth (John 14:6). The mustard seed was the smallest herb-producing (i.e., garden plant) seed used at that time in Israel. Rather than accommodating the ignorance of His audience, as some writers suggest, Jesus frames His parable within that context.

Secondly, He speaks proverbially, using a figure of speech common at the time to communicate the idea of insignificant smallness. You don't need a degree in botany to understand that. Subconsciously, we use similar communication techniques. For example, have you ever been "so hungry you could eat a horse"? Have you ever met someone so rich he has "tons of money"? Ever met someone "as tall as a house"? Haven't we seen figures of speech in the Bible "a million times"? Irony bonus: We use these expressions "all the time."

- Read Matthew 17:20, and describe how He uses the same figure of speech.

Now that we've verified that Christ would never say anything inaccurate and that the Bible does not contain errors, I want you to see the Old Testament's prophecy about the regional inauguration of the kingdom of heaven.

- Read Micah 5:2 and Matthew 2:6. What can you tell about the regional inauguration of the kingdom of heaven in mystery form?

- Read Ezekiel 38:23. What can you tell about the universal influence of the kingdom of heaven in mystery form?

The natural growth of a mustard seed produces a shrub as tall as thirty feet. In this parable, the tree towers over all the others in a fictitious garden and becomes large enough to provide security, shelter, and sustenance for birds.

- Read Daniel 4:20–22, and list features of the other metaphorical tree that symbolizes universal influence.

Other nations benefited from the dominance of ancient Babylon. However, any comparison with the mustard tree must end here because God chopped this Babylonian tree and established others. Although not pictured in plant imagery in the Bible, Medo-Persia, Greece, and Rome also had universal influence.

Here's a more recent example of small turned worldwide: A group of 102 pilgrims and thirty crew members boarded the *Mayflower* in the year 1620 to reach what would become the land of the free and the home of the brave. America's universal influence today resembles a tall tree that provides security, shelter, and sustenance to many. We don't know how long this tree will stand. World superpowers rise and fall according to God's determination, but the proverbial mustard tree will last forever.

- According to 2 Samuel 7:13 and Luke 1:33, what is the duration of Jesus's reign?

_____

_____

_____

_____

Born-again believers in Christ belong to the only eternal institution that exists. The company you started has a shelf life (remember names such as Pan Am, Enron, Circuit City, and Tower Records?). One day your fishing club will dismantle. Nations' parliaments and congresses will cease to exist eventually.

On the other hand, Jesus advances His eternal kingdom through church saints, the people He commissioned to proclaim the message. What started regionally, in a small province of the Roman Empire, has ballooned and will continue to expand to influence the world. Not only do we get to witness this growth, we also get to participate in it, which leads us to the parallel parable.

DAY 2: LOCAL START FOLLOWED BY GLOBAL SCOPE (MATTHEW 13:33)

Growing up, Jesus would have seen His mother make bread exactly as He described in the parable of the leaven. Although other parts of Scripture associate leaven with evil, the parable of the tares already summarized the activity of Satan during the King's temporary absence.

This one-verse parable teaches the same concept as the mustard tree—namely, the unstoppable expansion of the kingdom of heaven—but because of the permeation character of yeast, this one seems to focus on transformational growth at the micro and macro aspects.

We can apply that change to individual members of the kingdom of heaven (the micro level). Because Jesus lives in the heart of every born-again believer, He permeates every aspect of your life: body, soul, will, emotions, and intellect. Why do you think Paul instructs the Roman believers to "not be conformed to this world, but be transformed by the renewing of your mind, so that you may prove what the will of God is, that which is good and acceptable and perfect" (Romans 12:2)?

We resist this sanctification process often, but our rebellion does not affect the growth of the kingdom at the macro level; it just hurts our conscience because as people who have been transformed, we don't fit the mold of the world anymore. We don't think, feel, or behave like non-members of God's kingdom.

Jesus wants His listeners to understand the progressive transformation at the macro level of the kingdom. After the forerunner announced the arrival of the King, the Messiah began His ministry locally, never crossing the borders of Israel. Because the nation rejected Christ, He postponed the establishment of his millennial reign to allow people from every other nation admittance to heaven, inflating the scope of His kingdom.

- Chart the leavening of the kingdom of heaven (its permeation in the world) according to the following verses:

Matthew 28:19:

John 14:12:

Acts 1:15–16:

Acts 2:8–11:

Acts 2:41:

As leavening agents, the believers in the early church disseminated the kingdom by sharing the good news with relatives and friends. From that time, the gospel made its way to Africa through Philip (Acts 8), to Europe through Paul (Acts 16), and to Asia through Thomas (according to the history books). Since then, church saints have perpetuated the process, spreading the kingdom of heaven on every continent.

Because of the rapid secularization of Western culture, you may think that Christianity has lost its leavening effect and that its days are numbered. Nothing can be further from the truth. Even though North America and Europe have long ceased to function as "Christianity hubs," apparently God has shifted the fermenting of His kingdom to what some call the Global South.

Observer of world religions Philip Jenkins identified this shift. In his book *The Next Christendom: The Coming of Global Christianity*, he predicts that "by 2050, 72 percent of Christians will live in Africa, Asia, and Latin America."[7] He quotes Philip Yancey tracing this development: "As I travel, I have observed a pattern, a strange historical phenomenon of God 'moving' geographically from the Middle East to Europe, to North America, to the developing world. My theory is this: God goes where He is wanted."[8]

You may disagree with Yancey's last sentence (and rephrase it by stating "God goes where *He wants*"), but you can't ignore the obvious: what started small and local two millennia ago has turned into a global movement that will continue to expand despite opposition and neglect, even if God moves the focus of permeation around the continents. This leavening will reach a climax in the millennial kingdom when the King of kings and Lord of lords returns to earth in full display of divine majesty.

- Read the following passages and describe the global scope of God's kingdom, especially after the return of Christ.

Daniel 7:13–14:

Micah 4:1–2:

Psalm 22:27:

---

7. Philip Jenkins, *The Next Christendom: The Coming of Global Christianity*, 3rd ed. (New York: Oxford University Press, 2011), xi.
8. Jenkins, *The Next Christendom*, 1

We long for those days because we live in the inter-advent period when Satan has limited autonomy, according to the parable of the tares. In the time between the rejection and return of Christ, the mystery form of the kingdom, after His ascension, Jesus lives in the hearts of believers (our hope of glory [Colossians 1:27]) and at the same time sits on His throne in heaven.

Rather than standing by idly dreaming about that glorious day, we should wait actively, following God's program for kingdom expansion. We do that by influencing the world, just like leaven penetrates and transforms dough.

Let me borrow another culinary metaphor from Christ: subjects of His kingdom "are the salt of the earth" (Matthew 5:13), who season the world with the knowledge of Jesus. We insert Him where His name has not been proclaimed yet (or needs to be preached again).

Don't fall for the misconception that the United States is not a mission field. We, along with our European brothers and sisters, live in the most secular parts of the world. The Bible Belt needs the gospel as much as the Resistant Belt (how missiologists have nicknamed the 10/40 window).

God has placed you in a post-Christian society by His providence, for the purpose of advancing His kingdom, which moves from regional inauguration to universal influence, from a local start to global scope.

- Read Matthew 13:34–35 and Psalm 78:2, and explain how Jesus's teaching technique fulfills the Old Testament prophecy.

On March 29, 2021, the Gallup Institute showed that church membership fell below 50 percent in the United States for the first time since 1973.[9] This steady decline may tempt you to think that an increasingly godless culture can halt God's purposes. Not according to Jesus. Giant corporations may boycott Christian values, but they can't stop the growth of His kingdom. Lawmakers may legislate immorality, but they can't slow the advancement of His kingdom. Civic leaders may imprison pastors and fence their churches to prevent people from entering the building, but they will never shut down the progress of the kingdom of heaven.

---

9. Jeffrey M. Jones, "U.S. Church Membership Falls Below Majority for the First Time," Gallup, March 29, 2021, https://news.gallup.com/poll/341963/church-membership-falls-below-majority-first-time.aspx.

Morally deteriorating cultures provide excellent opportunities for us to ferment the world with truth. We may lose our lives, livelihood, or freedom, but like the apostles, we thank God for the honor of suffering shame for His name (Acts 5:41).

The Christian movement had humble beginnings; today it suffers abuse, oppression, neglect, and persecution, but it will take over the world, literally, at the return of Jesus.

SIGNPOST 6

GOD STILL SATISFIES
(MATTHEW 13:44–52)

DAY 1: THE VALUE OF YOUR SALVATION (MATTHEW 13:44–46)

A few years ago, I learned an important principle in stewardship: your bank statement will tell you what you value the most in life. How you spend your money reveals much about what you esteem. Jesus stated this principle like this: "where your treasure is, there your heart will be also" (Matthew 6:21).

He teaches something similar in the next two parables in Matthew 13 by using concepts such as "treasure" and "great value." The Gospel writer hints that Jesus offered the next three kingdom illustrations to the disciples only (see vv. 36 and 51). He groups the next two stories by this theme and repeats the judgment motif in the last one.

Let's review what we learned so far: The parable of the sower symbolizes the proclamation of the kingdom. The tares among wheat represent opposition to the kingdom. The mustard seed and leaven illustrate the expansion of the kingdom.

In this lesson we will see that, just as He did with the disciples, Jesus helps us assign to the kingdom of heaven its appropriate worth. The next two parables communicate the estimation of the kingdom, and the dragnet teaches the purification of the kingdom.

The story of the hidden treasure and the costly pearl parable feature men who gladly liquidate their possessions to secure their newfound wealth. Far from suggesting that the kingdom can be purchased, Jesus teaches His listeners (and every future reader) the appraisal of our so great a salvation (Hebrews 2:3), indeed an incomparable treasure. Rather than lament coexistence with evil, widespread rejection, opposition, and perceived low influence, subjects of the King of kings should hold the kingdom of heaven in incalculable esteem.

Here's how Jesus illustrates this principle in the picture of the hidden treasure: The fictitious man either found the unspecified riches while plowing the ground of his boss, or he stumbled upon it as he crossed someone's land. He hid the treasure back and purchased the entire field because legal ownership of the land would entitle him to possess the treasure. The man would have disclosed his finding to the seller.

Imagine yourself in a similar situation: Somebody hires you to fix a sprinkler system, and you discover a deposit of coal under the ground while on the job. Integrity demands that you notify the person who hired you, the newest millionaire in the neighborhood. The homeowner would not sell the property, unless he failed to recognize the value in the riches you found.

A basic principle of economics states that people ascribe a monetary value to the goods they appreciate. You pay less than a dollar for microwave popcorn, but you cough up ten dollars for the popcorn and soda at the movie theater because, at that time, you cherish the comfort of enjoying the big screen while munching on salty kernels.

Notice that Jesus says nothing about the interaction between the finder of the treasure and the owner of the field. Because Christ would never teach divine truth while condoning shrewd business practices, we can conclude that the fictitious landowner did not see the value in the treasure and preferred to cash in the profit from the sale of his property.

- Read Matthew 16:1, and describe the attitude of the Pharisees and Sadducees toward the proverbial treasure in their field.

The self-proclaimed religious authority in Israel at the time of Jesus failed to appreciate Him properly, like many people today who want nothing to do with Christ because they crave the popularity that accompanies those who mock God. They do not treasure the kingdom of heaven. In fact, they scoff at what we do as a waste of time and resources.

- Contrast this view with the biblical perspective in 2 Corinthians 4:7 and Ephesians 1:18.

- Read Hebrews 11:24–26 and Psalm 16:5, and describe how Moses and David assigned proper value to their position as members of God's family. In a few words, articulate your estimation of the kingdom of heaven.

In the next short parable, Jesus illustrates the same lesson but now uses the image of a costly pearl. Presumably, the first man discovered the gemstone accidently, but the fictitious merchant went to great lengths to obtain the object of his desire.

By specifying this man's effort, Christ does not intend to validate the so-called seeker movement. Let's see why.

- According to Paul in Romans 3:11, who seeks God?

_____

_____

_____

- What does God's assessment of the human heart in Genesis 6:5 tell us about people's ability to seek Him?

_____

_____

_____

Let me show you an example of how God draws people to Him. Luke writes about a man in Jerusalem whose name was Simeon,

> and this man was righteous and devout, looking for the consolation of Israel; and the Holy Spirit was upon him. And it had been revealed to him by the Holy Spirit that he would not see death before he had seen the Lord's Christ. And he came in the Spirit into the temple; and when the parents brought in the child Jesus, to carry out for Him the custom of the Law, then he took Him into his arms, and blessed God, and said, "Now Lord, You are releasing Your bond-servant to depart in peace, According to Your word;
> For my eyes have seen Your salvation,
> Which You have prepared in the presence of all peoples,
> A LIGHT OF REVELATION TO THE GENTILES,
> And the glory of Your people Israel. (Luke 2:25–32)

Just like in the parable of the costly pearl, Simeon represents someone who found a treasure of a great price because of divine initiative. As a result, he esteemed his salvation more than his own life.

Once again, Jesus omits some details. Whether the merchant harvested pearls from the bottom of the sea or hired someone to do it, the story focuses on the worth of the object found. Like the previous man, the merchant appraised the kingdom of heaven infinitely higher than his possessions.

The lesson of these parables emerges clearly: we should assess the kingdom of heaven in such a way that the cost of discipleship pales in comparison. Therefore, the two parallel short stories describe total abandon and complete surrender. They illustrate believers who renounce the world to follow their Savior no matter the cost, like the disciples who left their nets to heed the call, "Follow Me, and I will make you fishers of men" (Matthew 4:19). That's the kind of man I want to be: willing to forsake my life for my Lord.

Christ expects no less from you. Why would you not deny yourself to follow the One "who gave Himself for us to redeem us from every lawless deed, and to purify for Himself a people for His own possession, zealous for good deeds" (Titus 2:14)? Are we going to hold back from the One who was pierced for our transgressions and crushed for our iniquities (Isaiah 53:5), the One who traded our sin for His life?

- Read Philippians 3:7–8, and describe Paul's priority system.

- According to Galatians 1:14, what has he left behind for the sake of Christ?

The apostle relinquished recognition and popularity with his peers to endure ill treatment, beatings, arrest, and eventually martyrdom by beheading. Why? Because he considered his salvation infinitely more valuable than anything this world offers. Gladly, he absorbed the cost of following Christ.

How much do you cherish your salvation? What are you willing to sacrifice for the honor of following your Savior? Would you give up your unalienable rights? Your comfort, pride, and perceived security?

DAY 2: GOD'S ASSESSMENT OF YOUR SALVATION (MATTHEW 13:47–52)

Jesus offers another reason His followers should ascribe priceless value to the kingdom of heaven. His next illustration mirrors the parable of the tares; He even repeats the same sentences word for word (vv. 42 and 50). The disciples, most of whom were fishermen, could not have missed this one. Christ gives them the image and the interpretation.

The expression "fish of every kind" symbolizes every person. No one can untangle from this kingly dragnet (another reason not to confuse the kingdom with the church). No person stands outside of the rule of the Christ; remember the concepts of universal influence and global scope from the mustard seed (vv. 31 and 32) and leaven parable (v. 33).

Unbelievers may think that because they reject Christ now, they will be able to opt out of this proverbial dragnet, but the divine fishing gear will catch everyone for the sorting. Neutrality with Jesus is only illusory; every person will face Him, either as Savior or Judge.

Angels will separate born-again believers (the righteous) from the wicked at the end of the age. Repeating the eschatological theme from verses 36–43, Jesus mentions the angelic agents of judgment again. They will place believers in the metaphorical containers, in the safety and comfort of God's eternal forgiveness.

- Read 1 Peter 4:12, and compare the image of fire that believers face against the fire that awaits unbelievers.

Fellow member of the heavenly kingdom: Jesus secured your eternal rest. He saved you by Himself (you contributed nothing to your salvation), for Himself (you belong to His family now), and from Himself (He will spare you from future judgment).

Tragically, unbelievers will experience both the fires of tribulations in this life and the eternal flames of eternal condemnation, which this parable pictures with the image of a furnace again. The plight of our friends who are still considered "bad fish" should keep us awake at night, pleading for their lives. We, who once were enemies of God and value our salvation so highly, should inform them that God still transforms the wicked into the righteous, bad fish into good ones.

- Read Romans 3:22, and describe God's kindness. What does God offer to anyone who comes to Him? According to Philippians 3:9, what is the basis for this divine favor?

- According to 2 Corinthians 5:21, what has God done so that sinners can become His righteousness?

Jesus concludes these short parables by revealing a third feature of the kingdom that highlights the incalculable value of our salvation.

In verse 51, Matthew does not suggest Jesus needs information from the disciples. His question launches the application, which He offers in the next verse, also in comparison format. The expression "all these things" refers to the mysteries of the kingdom of heaven: the seven parables in Matthew 13, the understanding of which God granted to the disciples and to every reader of the Gospel of Matthew (see 13:10). They now know the revelation, dissemination, opposition, expansion, estimation, and purification of the kingdom.

Christ used the word *scribe*, the Greek term *grammateus* (from which we get the word *grammar*), to describe Jewish religious teachers, many of whom spent all day copying manuscripts. His disciples did not have this official designation or job description recognized by the religious establishment, but Jesus commissioned them to preach the kingdom to the house of Israel first (Matthew 10:6–7).[10] In order to accomplish the task faithfully, they needed to explain to their Jewish countrymen that the kingdom of heaven had been predicted in the Old Testament, the mystery form concealed but now revealed by the King Himself.

Modern-day disciples do the same when we recognize the priceless character of our salvation, a treasure too precious for us to keep to ourselves. We have no risk of losing it, so we might as well share our most prized possession with as many people as possible.

When you share the gospel, you speak from the position of one poor in spirit (Matthew 5:3), who found redemption and forgiveness, "according to the riches of His grace which He lavished on us" (Ephesians 1:8). Open your treasure chest so others can see the riches they can gain in Christ. Here's how to do it.

What you value the most comes out of your mouth naturally because, according to Jesus, the mouth speaks out of the overflow of the heart (Matthew 12:34). If you value your family the most, guess who you're going to talk about continually? If you consider yourself the greatest gift you have, the world will see your self-centeredness. Nobody wants to associate with self-centered people.

But if you treasure Christ above all, no one will have to guilt-trip you into evangelism. You will talk about Him so much that the haters of God will run from you, slander you, or plot against you. Like the apostles, you will cause "no small disturbance concerning the Way" (Acts 19:23). Others will come to hear more about your Savior, whom you revere more than life. They will want to find Jesus like the men in the two previous parables.

- How does Revelation 11:10 describe the evangelism ministry of the two witnesses or prophets? Has anyone ever asked you to stop bothering them with the gospel? If so, describe the situation.

---

10. Chronologically, the commissioning of the disciples in chapter 10 happened after chapter 13.

That's how you apply the knowledge of the mysteries of the kingdom.

The Bible asks you now, Have you understood these things? Then put your treasure on display. Tell others about your most prized possession. Bring out of your treasure things new and old.

PART THREE

HIS REGAL MISSION

SIGNPOST 7

JESUS STILL SHEPHERDS
(MATTHEW 13:53–58)

DAY 1: TRUTH SURPRISES (MATTHEW 13:53–56)

Once in a while I pick up a book that makes it to my all-time favorite category, aside from the Bible. I knew I had a masterpiece in my hands when I read the following words in *The Preacher's Catechism* by Lewis Allen: "Preachers who don't commit to keeping on learning will end up saying the same things in the same way."[11] A preacher himself, Allen had my heart hooked when I read, "We want response, growth, revival, and maybe plenty of affirmation along the way. Some preachers do get that. But they are the exceptions."[12]

I kept turning the pages because the author took me back to my seminary days when I dreamed about reaching the world for Christ. I had visions of cooperating church members, eager to listen to me and to apply the timeless truth of Scripture, ready to shower their shepherd with affirmation and gratitude. But when I planted a church in San Diego, California, reality confronted me with the truth.

Before I came to Grace Baptist Church, my former senior pastor, Dr. David Jeremiah, told me I was about to start the most critical season of my life. He didn't need to elaborate; I knew he was alerting me about the opposition that afflicts those who desire to preach God's Word faithfully. I wish seminaries would offer courses on how to handle rejection and criticism. If I ever teach such a class, I will use what I consider the textbook on the subject: Joel Beeke's and Nick Thompson's *Pastors and their Critics*.[13]

Criticism should not surprise us. Paul warned a rookie pastor, "Suffer hardship with me, as a good soldier of Christ Jesus" (2 Timothy 2:3). But if you think rejection only burdens ministers, listen to how the apostle broadens this warning: "all who desire to live godly in Christ Jesus will be persecuted" (2 Timothy 3:12), which means your identification with Jesus puts a target on your back. The world hates the truth you represent.

---

11. Lewis Allen, *The Preacher's Catechism* (Wheaton, IL: Crossway, 2018), 17.
12. Allen, *The Preacher's Catechism*, 48.
13. Joel Beeke and Nick Thompson, *Pastors and Their Critics: A Guide to Coping with Criticism in the Ministry* (Phillipsburg, NJ: P&R Publishing, 2020).

- Read John 15:20, and elaborate on the passages above.

_____

_____

_____

_____

In this chapter, I want to show you three features of this identification with Christ that I hope will encourage you to draw closer to your precious Savior. The three products of truth in the closing remarks of Matthew 13 will cause repulsion from some people but will draw you closer to God.

As he concluded the kingdom parables, Matthew presents Jesus in another teaching capacity. This time the King spends time in Nazareth, where He grew up. The Gospel writer does not specify the content of Christ's sermons in the synagogues, but we know that whatever Jesus says is true because He is the truth (John 14:6). The narrative shows people's reactions, the first of which is a surprise.

The Nazarenes did not deny Jesus's authority and supernatural power. They had a hard time associating them with someone who had an ordinary upbringing, without a sophisticated background or royal blood; their description of Christ as the Son of the carpenter revealed their ignorance about the Lord's Davidic, royal descent. Furthermore, by naming His mother and siblings, the people of Nazareth also demonstrated a lack of understanding of Jesus's dual nature.

A clear grasp of the foundational doctrine of Jesus's dual nature, which theologians describe as a "hypostatic union," is essential to our faith. Let's go over this truth. Jesus is fully human, the adopted Son of the carpenter. At the incarnation, "the Word became flesh, and dwelt among us" (John 1:14). In order to dwell among people, He had to become one of us, even though He has always existed from eternity past. Also, because He came to the earth to die for sinners, Jesus had to have flesh and blood, because you can't nail a disembodied spirit on a cross. Before His resurrection, He displayed human limitations such as hunger and fatigue.

- Read Philippians 2:6–7, and describe how Jesus emptied Himself. Has He ever given up His divinity?

_____

_____

_____

_____

- Describe Christ's dual nature according to the scene in Matthew 17:1–9.

_____

Jesus is also fully God. He articulated this doctrine with these words: "I and the Father are one" (John 10:30). Along with the Holy Spirit, the Son shares the same essence and divine nature with the Father. Consider the following texts: Jesus participated in creation (John 1:1). He existed before Abraham (John 8:58), and in "Him all fullness of Deity dwells in bodily form" (Colossians 2:9). In fact, "He is the radiance of His glory and the exact representation of His nature" (Hebrews 1:3).

Proper understanding of the identity of Christ separates true Christianity from cults. You cannot claim to be a born-again Christian (a member of the kingdom of heaven) unless you can correctly answer the questions of the Nazarenes in verses 55–56. Tragically, many believers fumble with this doctrine.

- Read Matthew 16:16–18 and articulate Christ's nature. What promises does Peter's confession elicit from Jesus?

- Read John 10:27, and describe how to identify His people. Are you in the fold?

The Nazarenes of Matthew 13:53–56 had God incarnate in their synagogue explaining truth to them, yet they missed Him. Can you think of anything more unfortunate?

Their surprise represents common reactions today. The gospel is surprisingly simple; a four-year-old can articulate it. The simplicity of the cross astonishes the human mind because the natural man suppresses the truth in unrighteousness (Romans 1:18). The message of the crucified God crushes human pride.

Our flesh craves the credit that belongs to Christ alone. Therefore, we wonder, "Can the carpenter's Son put me in the right relationship with my Maker, or is this something I can do on my own?"

Truth surprises but also saves, according to Jesus. He promises, "you will know the truth, and the truth will make you free" (John 8:32).

• Read Romans 6:4, and describe how we can celebrate the liberating power of truth.

_____

_____

_____

_____

We have a different relationship with our sin after Christ has set us free. For example, if you used to embellish your stories to always make you the hero, you should lie no more. Make Jesus the protagonist of your life. If you bought the popular deception that other people's opinion of you determines your self-worth, ditch the deception and embrace the truth that your identity is anchored in Christ.

According to Jesus's visit to Nazareth, truth not only surprises, it also offends and condemns.

DAY 2: TRUTH OFFENDS AND CONDEMNS (MATTHEW 13:57–58)

Matthew uses the Greek word *skandalizo* (from which the word *scandal* originates) to describe the reaction of the Nazarenes. They stumbled when they should have rejoiced. Here's why: The people who witnessed Jesus's earthly ministry saw a great light, "AND THOSE WHO WERE SITTING IN THE LAND AND SHADOW OF DEATH, UPON THEM A LIGHT DAWNED" (Matthew 4:16). Now, the distinguished Resident returned to Nazareth to illuminate the place with divine truth. Sadly, and to their own condemnation, their hardened hearts eclipsed the glare of the son.

What could He have done or said to trigger their anger? Luke gives us a clue. Following His temptation in the desert, in His first visit, Jesus

> came to Nazareth, where He had been brought up; and as was His custom, He entered the synagogue on the Sabbath, and stood up to read. And the book of the prophet Isaiah was handed to Him. And He opened the book and found the place where it was written,
>
> > "THE SPIRIT OF THE LORD IS UPON ME,
> > BECAUSE HE ANOINTED ME TO PREACH THE GOSPEL TO THE POOR.
> > HE HAS SENT ME TO PROCLAIM RELEASE TO THE CAPTIVES,
> > AND RECOVERY OF SIGHT TO THE BLIND,
> > TO SET FREE THOSE WHO ARE OPPRESSED,
> > TO PROCLAIM THE FAVORABLE YEAR OF THE LORD"
>
> And He closed the book, gave it back to the attendant and sat down; and the eyes of all in the synagogue were fixed on Him. And He began to say to them, "Today this Scripture has been fulfilled in your hearing." (Luke 4:16–21)

The warm welcome turned cold as soon as He confronted them with their hardness of heart, at which point, "all the people in the synagogue were filled with rage as they heard these things; and they got up and drove Him out of the city, and led Him to the brow of the hill on which their city had been built, in order to throw Him down the cliff. But passing through their midst, He went His way" (Luke 4:28–30).

Shockingly, Christ returned to the place after He told the kingdom parables. (Matthew records Jesus's second visit to Nazareth.) By this time the people had heard of His miracles, which is probably the reason they didn't try to kill Him again, and their anger had subsided, but they still missed the truth.

The mention of Jesus's half brothers and sisters confirms two facts: First, Mary did not remain a virgin perpetually, like the Roman Catholic Church teaches. Second, His listeners employed a tactic common even to this day to deflect responsibility. They asked the wrong questions. The occupation of His adopted father and the names of His siblings have no relevance to anybody's eternal destiny. They should have asked another question, "Is His message true?" If so, then truth has a claim on their lives.

Likewise, people today offer irrelevant justifications for their rejection of the truth that offends their sin. Let me list some of them: "The Bible contains many mistakes." (Ask the person making this affirmation for one example, and watch his or her argument crumble.) "The pastor's beard and his shiny head distract me." "The social distancing thing bothers me." (This one featured in the early days of the COVID-19 pandemic.) "I don't like the music." "The usher didn't shake my hand."

I remember a phone call from a man complaining about the stained glass behind the pulpit in my former church. He said the art distracted him, but I gave him a simple answer: "Focus on the truth coming from the pulpit, and the glare of God's Word will hide the supposedly ugly art."

Let's not dodge our responsibility to respond to the truth that offends. The color of your pastor's suit (or jeans) is irrelevant. You should ask the question, "Is the message true?" If it is, the heart issue that God's Word addresses should trump your sensibility.

The truth offends but also operates, like a surgeon who reveals a deadly disease prescribes lifestyle changes and performs open-heart surgery with care and precision. I'd rather be punched by the truth than caressed with a lie. I prefer being insulted by Jesus (like the Pharisees were) to being indulged by Satan. It is better for my soul to receive Scripture's assault on my sin than society's approval of it.

When you take this position your own culture will reject you and you will be like a prophet without recognition in his hometown. Consider yourself exceedingly blessed, for you are walking in the footsteps of your Savior.

Jesus addressed the denial of the Nazarenes with a proverb, which they heard before. He demonstrates that their unbelief did not surprise Him. His miraculous signs authenticated His message, but because they showed no regard for the message, He moved on.

Although Christ did not call fire from heaven on that occasion, He will hold those people, along with everyone who rejects Him, accountable for unbelief.

- According to Matthew 10:14–15, why will that generation of Nazarenes receive a harsher sentence than those from Sodom and Gomorrah?

- Why does Jesus condemn the people of Chorazin and Bethsaida in Matthew 11:21? What does that say about Jesus's ability to know both reality and potentiality?

The Nazarenes failed to acknowledge Jesus, not because of lack of evidence. The One who embodies truth spoke to them and validated His message with signs and wonders. They rejected Christ because of their rebellious, wicked hearts. Please don't suffer the same tragedy. The author of Hebrews warn, "Take care, brethren, that there not be in any one of you an evil, unbelieving heart that falls away from the living God" (3:12).

Times have changed since those days in Nazareth, but the wickedness in the human heart seems to have worsened. We live in a society where people refuse to acknowledge the truth, even though God has provided sufficient evidence of His nature and character.

- Read Romans 1:18–24, and answer the following questions.

What does God reveal from heaven, and how?

How has humanity responded to that divine revelation?

What are the consequences of truth suppression?

Our generation is witnessing God's condemnation of America (and the rest of the Western world), a judgment not of fire and brimstone, but the wrath of being given over to impurities for dishonoring bodies.

Our society wants you to think that a man pretending to be a woman, dressed in a demonic-looking, grotesque costume reading stories to children in public libraries represents progress. In reality, "Drag Queen Storytime" is the pouring out of divine judgment. From God's perspective, He "gave them over to degrading passions; for their women exchanged the natural function for that which is unnatural, and in the same way also the men abandoned the natural function of the woman and burned in their desire toward one another, men with men committing indecent acts and receiving in their own persons the due penalty of their error" (Romans 1:26–27). There is nothing liberating about the sexual revolution of our time.

Let me give you some good news: The truth condemns but also converts. The same God who pours His wrath by permitting people to wallow in their sin stands ready to forgive, restore, and cleanse. The situation in Nazareth was not hopeless. They knew where to find Jesus, even after His resurrection and ascension. In fact, His offer still stands today.

- Read John 4:14, and articulate the offer. Write the name of someone who needs to hear this offer today. Pray for him or her, and go share the good news.

Likewise, the situation in your hometown is not hopeless. You know where to find Christ. Our society has driven Him away from the public square, but He is omnipresent. Sadly, even some churches have pushed Him to the margin. But Jesus is the Lord of our churches. We do not take offense at Him. We lift Him up, even if doing so would cost our reputation with the moral revolutionaries of our day.

We don't mind enduring rejection by people because of Christ. What should terrify us is seeing people rejected by Jesus because of their unbelief.

Signpost 8

Jesus Still Seeks
(MATTHEW 9:35–38)

After revealing the mysteries of the kingdom of heaven to His disciples, Jesus sent the twelve, two by two, to proclaim the message to the lost sheep of Israel (Matthew 10:6). This first preaching tour would train them for the broader mission to all the nations after His resurrection and ascension (Matthew 28:19).

Matthew arranges his material by theme rather than chronology, but Mark provides the sequential link for what happened between the kingdom parables and the dispatching of the disciples turned apostles.[14] He reports that Jesus returned to Nazareth (see Matthew 13:53), but the people

> took offense at Him. Jesus said to them, "A prophet is not without honor except in his hometown and among his own relatives and in his own household." And He could do no miracle there except that He laid His hands on a few sick people and healed them. And He wondered at their unbelief. And He was going around the villages teaching. (Mark 6:3–6)

In this book, we will follow the consecutive order because I want to show you that Jesus used the parables of the kingdom to equip the first generation of men who would launch the Christian movement. Our generation, also commissioned to take the gospel to the world, now knows enough features of the kingdom of heaven to have renewed hope. Because we have learned these royal mysteries, we are better trained to honor Jesus's regal mission.

I also want you to see how Christ's compassion motivates Him to seek people. His enlisting of the twelve unveils more signposts to guide you through turbulent times. We will cover each one in the remaining chapters of this book.

- Read Matthew 13:53–58; Mark 6:1–7a; Matthew 9:35–38; and 10:1 (in this order), and describe the sequence of events in the life of Jesus.

---

14. The first of the five major discourses in Matthew is the Sermon on the Mount, chapters 5–7, which I plan to cover in another book. The missionary discourse in Matthew 10 happened after the kingdom parables, the third discourse.

Besides linking Jesus's second and third discourses, the last two paragraphs of Matthew 9 confirm the driving force behind His love for people, something Christians should reproduce.

• How can you duplicate divine compassion according to Paul in Ephesians 4:1 and 1 Corinthians 11:1?

Let's start by highlighting Jesus's motivation behind His search for the lost.

DAY 1: HIS INTENTION (MATTHEW 9:35)

Matthew describes Jesus's mission in an almost identical verse. The compassionate King "was going throughout all Galilee, teaching in their synagogues and proclaiming the gospel of the kingdom, and healing every kind of disease and every kind of sickness among the people" (Matthew 4:23).

• Read Luke 19:10, and explain what this repetition confirms about Christ's objective.

His intention is threefold.

Teaching

Matthew uses the Greek term *didaskon*, from which comes the English word *didactic*, to describe Jesus's first activity in the cities and villages. Synagogues started to appear during the intertestamental period. They were not temple replicas, but places where rabbis taught local congregations of Jews. During the time of Christ, officials of these learning centers had the habit of allowing itinerant teachers to explain the Old Testament to the locals.

• Read Luke 4:16–20, to verify how Jesus adopted this custom to reveal Himself to the Jews.

- According to Acts 17:1–3, why did Paul use the same strategy?

Evidently, the early church inherited the practice of gathering to hear a man teach the Word of God. The modern church perpetuated the habit because we want to honor Christ's intention to feed His people through sound doctrine. For this reason, Paul instructs Timothy that elders must be able to teach (1 Timothy 3:2). The apostle also clarifies the content of the teaching in the church: "All Scripture is inspired by God and profitable for teaching, for reproof, for correction, for training in righteousness; so that the man of God may be adequate, equipped for every good work" (2 Timothy 3:16–17).

Churches that teach anything else dishonor the legacy of Christ and of the apostles. We may discuss social issues, politics, and economics as long as we learn what God says about these matters in Scripture. Like Paul, we present the full counsel of God (Acts 20:27). A pastor-teacher should never volunteer his opinions from the pulpit. He must feed the sheep of Christ by explaining truth to them. I have a very simple job description: I teach my congregation what the Bible says, what Scripture means (God's Word says what it means and means what it says), and what the text requires of believers.

Jesus's teaching contrasted with the methodology of the scribes and Pharisees, who misunderstood and misapplied the Old Testament (and, therefore, confused the identity of Christ). He exposed their error in a common expression He used in the Sermon on the Mount: "You heard what was said . . . but I say to you." He means, "You have the wrong view of the Bible, but let me give you the correct one."

Proclaiming

Matthew defines the next directive in this ministry tour using the Greek term *kerusson* (translated "preaching" or "proclaiming"). The term describes the job of a herald, the steward of an authoritative message, someone who issues a public summons on behalf of a king. Paul instructs young pastor Timothy using the same term: "preach the word; be ready in season and out of season; reprove, rebuke, exhort, with great patience and instruction" (2 Timothy 4:2).

Think of an ancient messenger in the town square who unrolled a scroll and announced, "Hear ye, hear ye (or 'listen up, everybody'). The king has arrived victorious from the battlefield."

Likewise, Jesus proclaimed the message from the Father with equal authority. Elsewhere He said, "For I did not speak on My own initiative, but the Father Himself who sent Me has given Me a commandment as to what to say and what to speak" (John 12:49). Notice the content of the announcement. In Matthew 3:2, Christ's forerunner proclaimed the arriving King who would offer the kingdom, then Jesus repeated the short sermon, "Repent, for the kingdom of heaven is at hand" (Matthew 4:17) and elaborated that people must enter the kingdom through the narrow gate (Matthew 7:13).

• Read Acts 2:38, and identify the command and desired result in Peter's message.

• Read Acts 17:30–32, and identify God's command to all mankind and why everyone should heed, according to Paul.

The church must continue this legacy of proclamation because Christ still offers the kingdom to people. As ambassadors of Jesus, we don't merely suggest that people come to Christ. More than an invitation, we echo the summons from the Majestic Savior. Like Paul, we proclaim, "Be reconciled to God" (2 Corinthians 5:20).

Because many people don't think they need peace with God, we must balance our authoritative proclamation with compassion. In kindness, we must affirm that people are, by nature, alienated from the Creator, and unless they respond in faith to the call of salvation, they will suffer condemnation forever.

• Read Colossians 1:19–20, and describe how Jesus made reconciliation between God and man possible.

• Read 1 Corinthians 1:23–24, and identify the main content of our preaching, if we are to follow Paul as he imitates Christ.

Restoring

Next, Matthew uses the Greek term *therapeuon*, from which we get the English word *therapy*. The term communicates "reversal of a physical condition." Besides demonstrating Christ's power over disease and previews of kingdom realities (restoration of bodies), the healings throughout the cities and villages demonstrate His unique ability to reverse the curse of sin, started in Genesis 3.

The apostles also had miraculous powers that would authenticate their message (e.g., Peter in Jerusalem [Acts 3:6] and Paul in Lystra [Acts 14:8–10]). But those seem to have been exclusive to the apostolic age of the church (before the completion of the canon of Scripture).

None of us has the apostolic gift of healing. But while we may not be able to tell paralytics to "get up and walk," we can tend to people's spiritual wounds.

- What virtues can you demonstrate to others in the context of the local church, according to Galatians 6:1–2 and Ephesians 4:32, that promote spiritual healing?

We can pray for healing, but if God decides to withhold physical restoration, we ask Him for endurance, fully aware of the sufficiency of His grace (1 Corinthians 12:9).

DAY 2: HIS INCLINATION AND INSTRUCTION (MATTHEW 9:36–38)

In the last paragraph of chapter 9, Matthew describes Jesus's perception of the crowds using Greek terms for the people as "troubled," "harassed," "weary," "cast away," "mangled," and "dispersed." The author adds the picture of lost and scattered sheep, but most importantly, he wants his readers to understand that Christ's assessment of the multitude prompted divine compassion.

The Sermon on the Mount sheds light on the Lord's thought process. The men who claimed to be the leaders of Israel (the scribes and Pharisees) spiritually abused their followers. These false shepherds murdered people in their hearts by hating them (5:21–22), committed spiritual adultery (5:27–28), judged everybody else prematurely (7:1–2), and refused to forgive (5:14–15). When the compassionate Savior arrived, these hypocrites accused Him of blasphemy and affiliation with Satan. No wonder the crowds felt bruised and battered.

I am persuaded that the terms *distressed* and *dispirited* accurately describe our society today. What else do you expect when our culture neglects grace and embraces legalism (the religion of the Pharisees)? I am equally convinced that some of you are weary, heavy laden, bruised, and battered, not because you have false shepherds (you have imperfect pastors, for sure), but primarily because our society constantly leads people away from the true Shepherd, bombarding us with unbiblical ideas about how to deal with the stress of the times. "Cancel your offenders, withhold forgiveness, pursue punishment, and ignore reconciliation," demands the current worldly value system. The same unbiblical attitude demands that you point out the speck in your brother's eye while ignoring the log in your own. Many of you are weary because a log weighs much more than someone else's speck.

The Majestic Savior is the Good Shepherd who lays down His life for His sheep (John 10:11). He raised some undershepherds to gather the scattered sheep, tend to their wounds, feed them the nutritious Word of God, and lovingly rebuke them when necessary.

- Read 1 Peter 5:2–3, and outline the elders' job description. Write the name of one of your pastors or elders, and commit to praying for him this week. (I am sure he would not mind receiving an encouraging phone call from you).

Your pastors discharge their shepherding duties imperfectly but gladly. When they see your distress, they hurt for you because, generally speaking, their hearts align with Jesus's. Faithful elders desire nothing more than to imitate the Good Shepherd.

According to Matthew, Jesus offers the image of farming again. The analogy teaches the disciples to solve the problem of the hurting sheep. But rather than presenting a detailed plan, Christ unfolds the most effective strategy in the art of caring for distraught people.

Let me take you back to a familiar scene to understand His rationale.

The picture of a harvest refers to future judgment. Jesus elaborated on this image when he told the parable of the weeds and tares. (Remember, some people will be bundled, and others will be burned.) Christ wants His disciples to know that the Father draws people to Himself for the gathering in His barn, which represents heaven. However, the Lord's harvest experiences a continual shortage of workers. The scarcity is not due to bad management, but because of the labor-intensive, thankless, and unpopular nature of the work. Many people sign up for it but give up mid-harvest.

Interestingly, Jesus makes no mention of a recruiting campaign. Instead, He provides a much better solution, one that should always be the first option. Sadly, many consider prayer an emergency strategy only. What's the first thought that comes to mind when someone asks for intercessions? "What's wrong?" "What happened?" "Who died?" As if petitioning the Father were a strange habit.

Matthew quotes this instruction to the disciples immediately after he records Jesus's compassion. The obvious connection is that workers in the Lord's field need to operate from a compassionate heart. Otherwise, they will abuse, harass, and scatter the sheep (like the scribes and Pharisees). Compassion-less Christians (a hard concept to grasp) have no business working for God, because they do not accurately represent the heart of Christ.

If you struggle with this virtue, whether for unbelievers or your fellow believers, consider this thought: harvesting souls for the Lord is not the exclusive domain of pastors, teachers, elders, and deacons, but of every believer.

- Read, paraphrase, and apply the following passages:

Matthew 28:19–20:

Luke 24:45–49:

John 20:21–23:

Acts 1:8:

If you belong to the kingdom of heaven, you are in God's field. When you don't do your job, someone else will pick up the load, and that person could probably use some rest. Collect the tools today, and reproduce the compassion of your Savior. Start praying for God to raise workers, and soon He will place a burden in your heart for lost people.

I can't think of a faster way to kill a church than to ignore the command to pray for harvesters and the order to replicate Christlike compassion. All it takes is a slight shift in focus, whether manifested in the desire for acceptance or the personality of strong-willed church members. When that loss of focus happens, people default to their natural desires for self-fulfillment. They start quarreling because they didn't get their way. The gospel loses its prominent place, and the result is tragic.

We can prevent this tragedy in our churches by continually praying for a heart of compassion; a prayer-less congregation will easily get distracted by politics, current events, or secondary issues. But when each of us does our job as a laborer in the Lord's harvest, we allow our shepherds to care for distressed sheep. It takes no more than a generation for a church to lose its distinctiveness. It happened in Europe, it happened in Canada, and it's happening in the United States faster than you think. But if we claim identification with Jesus, we will seek the lost just like He does.

JESUS STILL SERVES
(MATTHEW 10:1–15)

DAY 1: THE DIVINE CHOICE (MATTHEW 10:1–4)

What do Queen Esther, King Saul, Judge Barak, Priscilla and Aquila, Martin Luther, Nicolaus Zinzendorf, William Wilberforce, William Carey, and Adoniram Judson have in common? They were ordinary people who God raised for extraordinary service.

Insert your name in that list.

God called us, His church, for extraordinary service, to represent the King of kings in a morally decaying, increasingly godless society. Because Jesus wants people to hear that His kingdom is at hand, He diffuses His compassion though His followers, who act as ambassadors of grace.

Jesus starts the scene in chapter 10 of the Gospel of Matthew by demonstrating God's answer to the prayer He just commanded the disciples to pray (9:38). His choice and commission of the apostles reveals His strategy for soul harvesting.

- Read Matthew 10:1–4, and list everything you can about each of the names in the list.

_____

_____

_____

_____

Let's look at the matter, the mode, and the men of Christ's divine choice.

The Matter

After empowering the twelve, according to Mark, Jesus sent them two by two (Mark 6:7). They received authority they did not possess naturally because His choice had nothing to do with their qualification. In fact, none of them qualified for soul harvesting; they were fishermen, a tax collector, and an insurrectionist, and one would betray Him. Therefore, Scripture proves that Christ alone equips His chosen workers.

Similarly, Jesus has given every believer His authority to proclaim the kingdom. Although we do not have the same powers as the first generation of disciples, we have everything we need—the complete and God-inspired work documented by some of them.

- According to John 15:16, what does He expect from His workers?

The Mode

Matthew identifies the disciples as apostles for the first time; he uses a Greek word that describes someone sent with a message and endowed with specific powers. The author of Hebrews uses the same word to describe Jesus as "the Apostle and high Priest of our confession" (Hebrews 3:1). Christ explains why: after His resurrection, when He commissioned the disciples to go to the nations, He said, "As the Father has sent Me, I also send you" (John 20:21).

The Father sent Jesus to redeem undeserving sinners. The King came to earth to offer the kingdom to people. He chose a group of twelve ordinary and unqualified men to proclaim His message. Future generations would perpetuate the process.

- According to Matthew 4:19, what analogy has Jesus used to teach this proclamation of the kingdom?

Eleven of them would launch the Christian movement after the resurrection and ascension of Christ. The body of doctrine they produced would serve as the foundation of the church (Ephesians 2:20).

- Read Revelation 21:14, and describe the perpetual reminder of the ministry of the apostles.

The Men

Matthew already mentioned five of these names: four in chapter 4 and his own conversion in chapter 9. Here, he presents the complete list in six pairs, perhaps to indicate the teams of two that Christ sent.

DAY 2: IMPERFECT PEOPLE ON A PERFECT MISSION (MATTHEW 10:1–4)

Peter always appears first in apostolic directories in Scripture (found also in Mark, Luke, and Acts), not because he was the first pope, but rather, he was first among equals, a natural leader. He receives more attention by the New Testament writers than any other apostle. Matthew records his birth name followed by the epithet Christ gave him: Petros (Cephas in Aramaic). His impulsiveness got him in trouble repeatedly, but his courage inspires, more so after Pentecost.

- What can you tell about Peter's personality by the way he started his famous sermon in Acts 2:14?

Some of you identify with Peter. You constantly regret talking too much, and if unrestrained, you take over the group discussion. God wired you as natural leaders, and He wants to use your personality for His glory. His power is made perfect in weakness (2 Corinthians 12:9).

The church needs more Peters to lead, move, and shake, to preach boldly, to make unpopular but biblical decisions and confront heresy. If you're a Peter, don't try to change someone made in the divine image; rather, allow God to mold your impetuous character for His glory.

Meet Andrew, whose name means "manly." He had the same profession as Peter but the opposite personality. He quietly and faithfully brought people to Jesus, including his brother.

- Read John 1:40–42, and describe how you might follow his example in bringing someone to Christ.

Andrew does not get the same attention as John, for example, but he didn't care. He just wanted to connect others to Christ and get away from the spotlight.

Some of you identify with him. You don't want the microphone (public speaking terrifies you), and you run from notoriety. The church needs Andrews to bring people to Jesus, not necessarily from a pulpit, but through personal relationships. I can't think of a better description of manliness in a culture that is so confused about the topic.

James (or Jacob), son of Zebedee, was a fisherman like his famous brother. His father's fishing business employed others, according to Mark 1:19–20, which suggests a comfortable financial position. Zebedee's wife was probably the Salome mentioned in Mark 15:40 and 16:1 (see also Matthew 27:56).

According to Luke, Herod had James killed (Acts 12:2), which makes him the first apostle to be martyred. Evidently, he posed a greater threat to the kingdom of darkness than Peter and John.

- Read Matthew 20:20–22, and describe James's family dynamics. Would your mother do something similar? Would you do anything similar for your sons?

Some of you are like James, John, Zebedee, and Salome. Your family serves together imperfectly but with excellence. Your dysfunctionality reminds you of His grace. You may argue in the car on the way to church and lose the fruit of the Spirit before the service begins, but your faithfulness, reliability, and dependability make you pillars in the community. Ministry would not be the same without each of you.

John, along with his less prominent brother, received the nickname "son of thunder" (Mark 3:17). He wrote the Gospel of John, three epistles, and the book of Revelation. He identifies himself as the disciple whom Jesus loved (John 13:23).

- What can you tell about John's relationship with Jesus from John 19:26 and 20:4?

He uses the word *love* thirty-nine times in his Gospel and thirty-four times in his three epistles (give or take, depending on the English translation you read), more than any other New Testament writer. He includes the word *truth* thirty-nine times, also more than his fellow New Testament authors.

Some of you identify with the apostle of love and truth. You are so committed to these two attributes that Jesus entrusts people to your care. He knows you always speak the truth in love to honor your Savior. The church needs more Johns.

Philip had a strange but common Greek name at the time, "lover of horses." John describes how this man first met Jesus: "The next day He decided to go to Galilee, and He found Philip. And Jesus said to him, 'Follow Me.' Now Philip was from Bethsaida, of the city of Andrew and Peter. Philip found Nathanael and said to him, 'We have found Him of whom Moses in the Law and also the prophets wrote: Jesus of Nazareth, the son of Joseph'" (John 1:43–45). Like Andrew, Philip enjoyed bringing people to Christ. In fact, the two shared this commitment.

- Read John 12:20–22, and describe Philip's strategy of leading people to Christ.

This disciple struggled to understand the identity of Jesus. Listen to the rebuke he heard from Christ: "Have I been so long with you, and yet you have not come to know Me, Philip? He who has seen Me has seen the Father; how can you say, 'Show us the Father'?" (John 14:9). A second-century bishop, Polycrates, documented that Philip took the gospel to Asia. Evidently, he got his Christology right.

Some of you identify with Philip. You may not have all the answers (in fact, you have many questions), but you delight in bringing people to the One who has them. The church needs more Philips. Too many people are quick to give answers, but like the lover of horses, "you keep the main thing the main thing." May your tribe increase.

Bartholomew, whose name means "son of Tolmai," also went by Nathanael. If he is the same one from John 1:47, Jesus describes him as an Israelite in whom there is no deceit.

Thomas, also known as Didymus, the "twin," received the unofficial title "doubting" because of his interaction with the other disciples after the resurrection.

- Read the interaction in John 20:24–25, and describe how some people today have a similar reaction when they hear about Jesus.

Jesus invited Thomas to touch the crucifixion wounds and followed up with a loving rebuke. Then Thomas uttered the confession the true church affirms to this day: "My Lord and my God!" (John 20:28).

Some of you identify with Dydimus. You think through every possibility before you commit. That's how God wired you—and He has not made a mistake. May I remind you, though, that the risen Christ will not appear to you? He has already provided unmistakable proof of His claims.

- Read Luke 1:1–4, and describe Luke's methodology for compiling his Gospel.

- Read 1 Corinthians 15:3–8, and identify undeniable evidence of the resurrection of Christ.

When Jesus clarified to the disciples that He wanted to go to Lazarus's funeral to raise him from the dead, everyone tried to dissuade Him because some people in Judea wanted Christ dead. Everyone except Thomas. He said to his fellow disciples, "Let us also go, so that we may die with Him" (John 11:16).

Some of you display the same courage. You will follow Jesus wherever He goes, even if it costs your life. May the Thomases among us rise, fully aware of their weak faith but willing to lead us in following Jesus at whatever cost.

Matthew (Levi) once again identifies himself by his old profession to remind his readers of God's grace in saving him from a life of dishonesty. Luke points out that Matthew left everything behind to follow Jesus immediately (Matthew 9:9).

Many Christians don't mind following Christ as long as they can hold on to some pet sins, their perceived comfort, or the illusion of financial security. The church needs more Matthews, men and women who don't hesitate to heed the call. I have met many believers like that; men and women who welcome God's process of weaning them from the world. They don't wait to see if He gives them a less demanding opportunity, unlike the man who asked Jesus if he could wait for his father to die and inherit his money before he would follow Him (Matthew 8:21).

James, the son of Alpheus (to be distinguished from the son of Zebedee), was not the brother of Jesus who wrote the New Testament book. Most likely, this man had another famous brother. Mark hints at that: "As He passed by, He saw Levi the son of Alphaeus sitting in the tax booth, and He said to him, 'Follow Me!' And he got up and followed Him" (Mark 2:14).

Thaddeus, also known as "Judas, son of James," according to the directory in Luke 6:16, does not get much attention from the New Testament writers, other than a line in John 14:22: "Lord, what then has happened that You are going to disclose Yourself to us and not to the world?" Some believe that this man authored the book of Jude, because he introduces himself as the brother of James (Jude 1).

Simon the Zealot (also known as the Canaanite) had this epithet because of a possible affiliation prior to coming to Christ with the Jewish nationalist group. This man probably expected a political Messiah who would overthrow Rome. The New Testament writers don't say anything more about him.

Judas Iscariot (literally, "Judah, the man from Kerioth"), also known as the son of Simon Iscariot (John 13:26), comes last in the list for obvious reasons. Jesus put him in charge of the ministry funds, but "as he had the money box, he used to pilfer what was put into it" (John 12:6). Obviously, Christ knew beforehand that Judas was a thief.

- Read Psalm 41:9 and Zechariah 11:12–13, and explain how these verses prophesy Judas Iscariot.

- Read John 13:21–27, and describe Jesus's kindness toward His traitor. What lessons can you learn from this scene?

Christ suffered betrayal; His followers will too; we are not above our master (see Matthew 10:24). Eventually, a business partner, a close friend, a spouse, or a child will break your trust. They may slander you, assassinate your character online, or sabotage your ministry.

The reality of betrayal should not surprise us. We live in a fallen world; sometimes even Christians default to worldly and carnal standards. But thank God for the example of Christ, whom we must imitate.

- How should you treat your traitor, according to the following verses?

Romans 12:19–21:

_____

_____

_____

John 18:22:

_____

_____

_____

1 John 3:15:

_____

_____

_____

Proverbs 25:21:

_____

_____

_____

DAY 3: THE DIVINE COMMISSION (MATTHEW 10:5–15)

Years ago, I went on a short-term mission trip to Manipur, India, where I walked through villages accompanied by a translator and a trainee. We would stop at mud huts and ask permission to share some good news. Not many people declined to hear about Christ, but several told me they would not mind adding Jesus to their collection of gods. The trainees would go back the next day to follow up and clarify the exclusivity of the gospel. According to Matthew 10:5–15, Jesus sent the apostles on a similar soul-harvesting mission.

- Read Matthew 10:5–15 and identify the details of this commission.

_____

_____

Jesus's commission of the original disciples has three aspects.

The Target

Jesus gave the disciples a clear objective: reach the lost sheep of Christ, the object of His compassion (see 9:36)—the Jews of His time. The people who claimed to be their shepherds, the scribes and Pharisees, failed in their pastoral duties, so Matthew shows his Jewish readers how much the True Shepherd cares about them. Jesus dispatches His messengers to call His fellow descendants of Abraham to the kingdom of heaven before anyone else.

- How does Matthew explain God's love and compassion for the Jews, according to the angelic announcement in Matthew 1:21?

- How does John describe the same love and compassion in John 1:11?

- How does Paul explain the same divine virtues in Romans 1:16?

This priority to the Jews does not mean gentiles belong in God's plan B; Matthew had already identified some non-Jews who received salvation (the Roman centurion, for example). Furthermore, Luke tells the story of Simeon, a devout Jew who took baby Jesus in his arms and praised God: "Now Lord, You are releasing Your bond-servant depart in peace, according to Your word; for my eyes have seen Your salvation, which You have prepared in the presence of all the peoples: A LIGHT FOR REVELATION FOR THE GENTILES, and the glory of Your people Israel" (Luke 2:29–32).

Christ focused this initial mission on the lost sheep of Israel, but after His resurrection, Jesus commissioned the disciples to reach the lost sheep of the nations. He instructed his disciples to "Go therefore and make disciples of all the nations, baptizing them in the name of the Father and the Son and the Holy Spirit, teaching them to observe all that I commanded you; and lo, I am with you always, even to the end of the age" (Matthew 28:19-20). Jesus explains the reason: "I have other sheep, which are not of this fold; I must bring them also, and they will hear My voice; and they will become one flock with one shepherd" (John 10:16).

- According to John 10:16, who are these sheep? What should you do, through your local church, to reach them for Christ?

_____

_____

_____

The Task

Jesus tells the disciples to preach the nearness of the kingdom. They were not allowed to say what people wanted to hear simply to appease the listeners or avoid opposition. Any content other than what Christ commanded would have made them guilty of dereliction of duty.

Likewise, we have the same marching orders. We do not have permission to water down the gospel to suit the taste of sinners. We don't compromise, even if the message costs our lives. Telling people Jesus wants to give them a successful life or that they can earn their salvation may generate popularity but leads people away from the true gospel. Most who embrace such a corruption of the good news experience bitterness when they encounter trials.

The twelve received authority to perform authenticating miracles. The author of Hebrews explains: "How will we escape if we neglect so great a salvation? After it was at first spoken through the Lord, it was confirmed to us by those who heard, God also testifying with them, both by signs and wonders and by various miracles and by gifts of the Holy Spirit according to His own will" (2:3-4).

Our current generation of disciples does not need to authenticate something that has already been confirmed. The complete Word of God is our credential. We can—and should—reproduce the compassion of Christ, but signs and wonders do not need to accompany our preaching.

Next, Jesus also tells the disciples exactly how to proceed. They would encounter people willing to hire them as personal healers or miracle workers, but the disciples had to avoid the corruption of serving God for money. This instruction would have been particularly relevant for Matthew and Judas Iscariot.

- Read 1 Timothy 3:3, and explain why elders must not be lovers of money.

How could someone speak of the free gift of God while charging for his or her mission? Instead, the disciples had to trust God for provisions and accept hospitality when offered.

Likewise, people should not charge a fee to preach the gospel. This does not mean the church should stop paying pastors. Paul instructs Timothy, "The elders who rule well are to be considered worthy of double honor, especially those who work hard at preaching and teaching" (1 Timothy 5:17). I get paid so I can focus entirely on the task, and woe to me if I preach not the gospel (1 Corinthians 9:16). Who should finance the ministry of kingdom proclamation in our day? Unbelievers will not pay to be reached for Christ.

The Terms

Jesus specifies the mission of the twelve. He instructs them to not insist when they encounter rejection, common in soul harvesting. Christ borrows from the common practice among Jews to leave Gentile dirt outside the houses. The worthiness of a household had to do with its willingness to receive the messenger of the King. Some people would recognize the nobility of the cause and provide lodging for the apostles, who would respond by recognizing it as divine provision, thus granting the greeting of peace. This does not mean God expects you to house everyone who claims to speak for Him. But when you do recognize someone as a legitimate servant you should acknowledge him or her.

According to Jesus, ultimately rejecting Him invites harsher judgment than the sin of Sodom and Gomorrah. Homosexuality can be forgiven and the homosexual restored, but someone who permanently refuses to turn to Jesus and declines the offer of salvation will spend eternity in what the Bible calls the lake of fire.

- According to Revelation 20:11–15, when will Christ judge unbelievers? What can you do to warn them now?

The statement from Jesus concerning leniency for ancient wicked cities shocked Matthew's original readers. Many of the Jews of that day did not consider themselves sinners, let alone worse than the Sodomites, who displayed their sins publicly.

Tragically, many believers quickly point out someone else's sin, especially if it becomes public, but they are slow to acknowledge (and quick to hide) their own transgressions.

According to biblical imagery, they point out the speck in everybody else's eyes without removing the log from their own (Matthew 7:3).

Finally, in a discourse that features compassion, Jesus affirms that there will be a day of judgment. He healed the sick, raised the dead, and sent apostles to do the same, but He highlighted divine compassion because He offers to withhold condemnation—the very definition of mercy.

Faithful gospel presentation must affirm the holiness of God. He saves because He is gracious, but He judges because He is holy. Correct gospel preaching also informs people what they're being saved from. When you came to Christ, He did not save you from yourself, bad habits, or even from the devil; He saved you from God (from His wrath), by God, and to God.

SIGNPOST 10

JESUS STILL SANCTIFIES
(MATTHEW 10:16–23)

DAY 1: HARDSHIP AWAITS BUT HOPE ASSURES (MATTHEW 10:16–20)

The twentieth century witnessed the greatest number of Christian martyrs in the history of modern missions. On January 23, 1999, members of a Hindu fundamentalist group, who vowed to eliminate Christianity from India, trapped Australian missionary Graham Stuart Staines along with his two sons, ten-year-old Philip and six-year-old Timothy, in their station wagon and set the vehicle ablaze. Staines had gone to India thirty-five years before to direct the Leprosy Home, an organization that ministered to tribal people in the city of Baripada, in the state of Odisha. Dara Singh, the man responsible for the murder, falsely claimed that Staines forced local Hindus to convert to Christianity.

In addition to demonstrating the compassion of Christ to the sick, the Australian missionary assisted with the translation of the Bible to the Ho tribe. Gladys, his widow, continued the Leprosy Home and in 2005 received the Padma Shree, the fourth highest honor a civilian can be awarded in India.

I can tell countless other stories that illustrate the high cost of ministerial faithfulness, but the Bible contains enough accounts for us to get the point. Scripture does not hide the dangers of soul harvesting. Paul states it clearly: "Indeed, all who desire to live godly in Christ Jesus will be persecuted" (2 Timothy 3:12).

- Read 2 Timothy 2:2, 8 and 3:1–5, and describe how Paul encouraged young Timothy.

Let's see what Jesus says about the dangers associated with faithfulness. He addresses the twelve apostles, but His words apply to every generation of disciples.

- Identify the animals in Matthew 10:16–20, and make initial observations about what human virtues or vices their behaviors represent.

By mentioning four animals, Jesus illustrates His warning about the hardships of ministry. Specifically, He presents two sets of contrasting features (serpents/doves and sheep/wolves). The image of sheep communicates vulnerability, helplessness, and gentleness. Sheep get lost, panic easily, and stampede at the slightest sign of danger. Imagine placing twelve of those animals close to a pack of predators; that's what Jesus did. He can do it because He has superior shepherding skills—and overpowers the wolves. Nothing they do escapes His control. Thus, He gives the disciples a picture of divinely ordained and controlled danger.

- What other features of our relationship with God can you identify in the following verses that feature images of sheep?

Psalm 23:1:

John 10:11, 14:

1 Peter 5:1–4:

Christians should expect constant attack from our spiritual predator, the one who seeks to devour (1 Peter 5:8). The devil orders his army to harm, slander, accuse, discourage, and persecute faithful followers of Jesus.

Because of the onslaught, the apostles would have been tempted to retaliate against persecutors, but later Paul clarifies to Timothy: "The Lord's bond-servant must not be quarrelsome, but be kind to all" (2 Timothy 2:24). Thus, the image of a dove reinforces Christ's expectation that His disciples be lowly, gentle, pure, peaceful, and harmless.

The mission of the apostles also required wisdom and discernment. Identifying the wolves demands the shrewdness of a serpent, which in this case has nothing to do with satanic craftiness—quite the opposite. The imagery speaks of attentiveness, prayerful vigilance, and prudence in movement.

To strengthen His command, speaking literally now, Jesus prescribes alertness against people, both on a political and religious front (represented by the courts and synagogues). The ministry of the disciples turned apostles would arouse suspicion in both the Romans and the Jews, but even though the disciples had to focus on the lost sheep of Israel (see v. 6), their trials would bring a good testimony to both Jews and Gentiles.

- Read Acts 4:1-3, and describe the type of attention and response Peter and John drew with the religious elite.

Paul experienced similar hardships, although he was not in this first group of apostles. Imagine his testimony to the Roman soldier to whom he was handcuffed while writing the letter to the Philippians, for example.

We have a similar mission today. Although we don't need to focus missionary efforts on Jews only, and we don't perform signs and wonders, we must embrace the timeless truth Jesus communicates here: faithfulness to Christ invites hardship, particularly in the form of opposition. Like He did with the disciples, He has not sent us on a vacation, but stationed you and me in dangerous places that require the vigilance and shrewdness of a serpent and the gentleness and humility of a dove.

Jesus comforts the disciples with the assurance that God would give them wisdom on how to testify before the courts, which would happen after the resurrection of Christ. He promises them that the Holy Spirit would speak through them.

- How does Luke describe this promise in Acts 1:8?

- Read Acts 4:19–20, and describe how you might exercise the same courage as Peter and John.

_____

_____

_____

- Read 2 Peter 1:20–21, and describe how the ministry of the Holy Spirit inspired the Bible authors.

_____

_____

_____

The same Holy Spirit who emboldened the disciples and equipped the authors of the Bible also indwells born-again believers in Christ (see 1 Corinthians 12:13). Therefore, you have the same promise of empowerment from God. His very presence in you gives you the hope necessary to navigate the dangers of faithfulness to Christ. However, this assurance should not encourage laziness. Remember, you must be vigilant like a serpent.

DAY 2: CONFLICT ABOUNDS BUT COMFORT ABIDES (MATTHEW 10:21–23)

Jesus introduces more principles about the dangers associated with faithfulness because He wants His disciples from every generation to know what to expect. When messengers of the kingdom obey Christ faithfully, they will encounter two more opposite realities: conflict abounds, but comfort abides.

The apostles' soul-harvesting ministry also featured conflict. Households would quarrel about the origin and truthfulness of their message. Jesus speaks of betrayal, death, and hatred, harsh realities for some believers even today. Many Islamic families punish members, sometimes by honor killings, for coming to Christ. In cults like Mormonism and Jehovah's Witness, coming to faith in the true Jesus invites anathema, disenfranchisement, and emotional shunning. In many of these cases, the cult leaders accuse the former member of being brainwashed.

Years ago, I led a man to Christ who had deep family traditions in Roman Catholicism. As we studied Scripture together, it did not take him long to see the contradictions of that system compared to biblical truth. When I asked if he was ready to be baptized, He told me, "My mother will die of a broken heart if she thinks I am leaving the Catholic Church." I shepherded him through his concern and sometime later baptized him. His mother did not die.

Here are some other examples of family conflict caused by faithfulness to Christ that I have seen in my years of ministry: the level of church involvement the saved spouse desires, tithing, principles by which to raise children, type of entertainment, consumption of alcohol or other substances, and conflict resolution. Rarely will the unbeliever in the house, whether a spouse, parent, or sibling, care to apply the biblical principles of forgiveness, restoration, lowliness, and selflessness.

It is not uncommon for unsaved family members to accuse believers of ruining Sunday morning plans, breaking family traditions, killing the fun in the marriage, and loving Christ more than their families. But even though conflict abounds in the life of a faithful believer, Jesus offers the balance. He contrasts the prediction of conflict with the promise of comfort and encourages the disciples to endure hardship and hatred on the promise of deliverance, which refers to eternal peace in glory. The time for conflict is significantly brief compared to an eternity of comfort and perfect fellowship.

- Read the following verses, and explain the comfort promised to believers.

Romans 5:3–5:

Romans 8:18:

2 Corinthians 4:17–18:

1 Peter 4:12:

- How would you comfort a fellow believer in distress using these passages?

_____

_____

_____

Let me give you a visual representation of that comfort, a concrete picture of an abstract idea. As John describes our eternal home, the New Jerusalem, he heard the voice of God: "Behold, the tabernacle of God is among men, and He will dwell among them, and they shall be His people, and God Himself will be among them, and He will wipe away every tear from their eyes; and there will no longer be any death; there will no longer be any mourning, or crying, or pain; the first things have passed away" (Revelation 21:3–4).

Conflict may abound in your life now because you follow Christ, but the God of all comfort abides in you. You should embrace the dangers of serving Him faithfully, confident that His enabling grace will equip you to endure.

We must differentiate, however, between true persecution and self-inflicted conflict. In other words, you should ask God to show you the real cause of the family conflict. Is it self-centeredness, for example? When you don't follow biblical standards, or when you refuse to give up a particular sin, God may put you in a crisis until you address the problem. I have experienced it in my own life. I see it frequently in other believers too.

As a final warning in this passage, Jesus gives the disciples perfect instructions about how they should respond to persecution. Interestingly, His prescription extends beyond the lifetime of the twelve all the way to the second coming of Christ. Two reasons explain that. First, Jesus validates the human need of self-preservation, although He commands total commitment, even at the point of death. There is nothing virtuous about desiring persecution. Martyrdom may result from faithfulness but should not be the goal. Once again, the shrewdness of a serpent would serve the disciples well. They would need wisdom to shut down operations in a particular city and move on.

Second, the twelve may not have canvased all the cities of Israel, but during the tribulation of the end times, missionary activity in the land will abound. At least twelve thousand Jews from each tribe will preach the gospel of the kingdom, according to Revelation 7:4–8.

You and I live in the period between the two advents of Christ. We have plenty of work to do. The work is hard, costly, lonely, and sometimes discouraging, but one day our eternal rest will start when He calls us home or when the Son of Man comes.

Let me conclude this chapter with a quote from Gladys Staines, the widow of Graham Staines, the man I mentioned in the beginning of this chapter. Speaking of the massacre that took the life of her husband and two boys, Gladys Staines said,

The Lord God is always with me to guide me and to help me try to accomplish the work of Graham, but I sometimes wonder why Graham was killed, and what also made his assassins behave in such a brutal manner on the night of the 22nd /23rd of January 1999. . . . It is far from my mind to punish the persons who were responsible for the death of my husband Graham and my two children. But it is my desire and hope that they will repent and be reformed.[15]

15. Morgan Lee, "Forgiver of Missionary Martyrdoms Wins India's Mother Teresa Award," *Christianity Today*, December 15, 2015, https://www.christianitytoday.com/news/2015/december /forgiver-india-mother-teresa-award-gladys-staines-martyrdom.html.

SIGNPOST 11

JESUS STILL STRENGTHENS
(MATTHEW 10:24–33)

DAY 1: ACKNOWLEDGE YOUR POSITION AND APPRECIATE YOUR PREPARATION (MATTHEW 10:24–31)

Jim Elliot, along with his four companions, Ed McCully, Roger Youderian, Pete Fleming, and Nate Saint, died in 1956 at the hands of men from the Huaorani tribe in Ecuador, whom the team tried to reach for Christ. Elliot wrote in his diary, "He is no fool who gives what he cannot keep to gain that which he cannot lose."[16] Those are words of someone who understands the cost of faithfulness to Jesus and paid the ultimate price.

The world needs mature spiritual leaders like Elliot. Our generation is so confused about its own identity that it has lost sight of what it means to lead. What else do you expect when you abandon divine principles? The year the pandemic began, 2020, provided opportunities for us to observe closely the leadership of civic magistrates. Tragically, public trust has plummeted. I wish I could say things looked better in the spiritual leadership department. In a general sense, they are not.

Thankfully, we can turn to our Bibles and learn from the Majestic Savior, the perfect, sinless leader. Like He did with the twelve disciples, today Jesus prepares us for spiritual leadership. Every believer in Christ serves in some spiritual leadership capacity. We are parents, spouses, friends, neighbors, community members, and so on.

- Read Matthew 10:24–33, and see if you can identify Jesus's strategy for spiritual maturity. How will you apply it in your life?

Jesus reminds His disciples about His position as Master and Teacher. His affirmation also clarifies the position of His followers. By presenting a timeless principle, He informs them that they would follow Him in suffering opposition and persecution. Elsewhere,

---

16. Elisabeth Elliot, *The Journals of Jim Elliot* (Grand Rapids, MI: Revell, 1978), 174.

Christ reminds them that they would also duplicate His godly influence: "Remember the word that I said to you, 'A slave is not greater than his master.' If they persecuted Me, they will persecute you; if they kept My word, they will keep yours also" (John 15:20). According to this principle, subjects of the kingdom of heaven will never rise above the Majestic Savior.

- According to Isaiah 14:13, who wanted to rise above God?

- What alternative does Paul recommend in 1 Corinthians 11:1? List specific ways you can achieve this goal.

Becoming like the Master means receiving similar treatment Jesus received, which He clarifies for the disciples by observing the accusation against Him. Specifically, the Pharisees associated Him with the "Lord of the Flies," the deity of Ekron (a town in the country of the Philistines), according to 2 Kings 1:2. The Jews equated this grotesque demon with Satan himself. The religious elite concluded, wrongly and tragically, that "He casts out the demons by the ruler of the demons" (Matthew 9:34). They would repeat the same blasphemy in Matthew 12:24.

True Christians know that insults and accusations of wrong motives afflict followers of Christ, precisely because people did the same to Him. The twelve disciples needed to acknowledge this truth because they would lead the early church.

- Read Matthew 12:50 and Galatians 6:10, and identify the blessing of belonging to the spiritual family of Jesus, even when such a position invites opposition.

We rejoice in our position and respond to opposition accordingly. People will second-guess your motives, but you are blessed with every spiritual blessing in the heavenly places in Christ (Ephesians 1:3). You are chosen in Him before the foundation of the world (Ephesians 1:4), predestined to adoption as sons and daughters (Ephesians 1:5), sealed in

Him with the Holy Spirit of the promise (Ephesians 1:13). The beatitudes of the Kingdom belong to you (Matthew 5:3–11). Furthermore, you are "dead to sin, but alive to God in Christ Jesus" (Romans 6:11). Because you are no longer in Adam, there is no condemnation for you (Romans 8:1), no matter the verdict from the court of public opinion.

We should consider it an honor to be opposed, insulted, criticized, and persecuted because of Christ. Mature, godly spiritual leaders do not panic when they receive insults and betrayal, but consider these experiences opportunities to demonstrate Christlikeness.

- How did the disciples learn this principle, according to Acts 5:41?

The apostles left this legacy of the true church. We stand on the shoulders of these giants of the faith, ordinary folks who rejoiced in their position, not above Christ, but in Him.

Training the disciples for godly spiritual leadership, Jesus taught them how to deal with the natural human response to danger and unknown circumstances. Why else would He command "do not fear" or "do not be afraid" three times in Matthew 10:24–33? He backs up these instructions by demonstrating the nature and character of God.

Jesus had already told the apostles they would encounter hardship and conflict in their mission. They would experience fear as a result, so He prepares them by issuing two commands, the first of which was to ignore the Pharisees who opposed Christ. The hypocrisy of these religious leaders would be exposed because nothing escapes the eyes of God, not even the secret chambers of the hearts of people who plotted evil against Him.

- How does the author of Hebrews articulate this principle, according to Hebrews 4:13?

God always exposes wrong motives and reveals godly intentions. People who seek self-interest (consciously or not) in serving Him can't fake for very long; eventually their self-centeredness surfaces. Conversely, if you enjoy a clean conscience, you should spend no time or energy reacting to every criticism, because that would distract from the real mission. The Lord will vindicate you in His time.

God would vindicate the disciples, even after some of them lost their lives.

Christ's followers should never hesitate to declare loudly and clearly His message, hence the image of a herald on a housetop for the entire village to hear in verse 27. They understood the analogy. Houses in that part of the world at that time had flat roofs designed for relaxation and sunbathing. They also served as platforms for important announcements.

Next, Jesus instructs the disciples to redirect their fear. People may be able to destroy the body, but God determines people's eternal destiny, either in hell or in heaven. (The word He used for hell was *gehena*, the city dump in Jerusalem at the time.) He makes the point that the wrath of God is so severe that any punishment inflicted by people would not even compare. Divine destruction, in this context, does not mean annihilation or the end of existence, which would actually end the misery of those suffering in hell.

Jesus wants the disciples to understand the holiness of God so that compassion for unbelievers would outweigh their instinct for self-preservation.

- Read Philippians 2:3, and describe how Paul's command confronts our natural tendencies.

_____

_____

_____

We should fear for our unsaved friends and family so much that the risk of being insulted (just like the Pharisees insulted Christ, calling Him the devil) should not cross our minds. What is the primary reason we don't share the gospel with others? Fear.

- According to Solomon in Proverbs 1:7, what is the beginning of knowledge?

_____

_____

_____

Of course, you don't want to upset people unnecessarily. As servants of Christ, we must live at peace with all people, "as far as it depends on you" (Romans 12:18). But we draw the line when it comes to biblical truth and people's eternal destiny. There shouldn't be any compromises there.

Jesus comforts the disciples with a simple illustration meant to communicate their need to not only fear God, but to trust Him. Here's what the imagery of the sparrows communicates: Compared to people, birds have a relatively low value, each priced at half an assarion (or a penny) at the time. The unit of value, a Roman copper coin, represented one sixteenth of a denarius, an average day's wage. God's sovereign care covers even these cheap creatures. How much more does He care for His image-bearers? He also ordains the seemingly insignificant and mundane details of people's lives, illustrated by the hairs on our heads.

By providing these examples, Jesus assures the disciples, whom He sent to the wolves, that God has ordained every circumstance of their lives. Birds reflect the creativity of the Creator, but they do not bear His image, like people do.

What part of "you are valuable" do we fail to understand? Do we need a clearer affirmation of divine love? Dear reader, you are precious to God. He values you so much that He takes care of the seemingly insignificant details of your life. He ordains them to fulfill His purposes, which may not be your first choice of events, but will cause you to trust Him and therefore mature spiritually.

- Read the following passages, and describe the value God ascribes to you.

Titus 2:14:

1 Corinthians 3:23:

1 Peter 2:9:

You should never fear people. When they rise against you, they trespass divine property, and that's a bad idea.

- Read Matthew 18:5–6, and articulate the level of personal involvement of Christ in the care of His people, the child illustrating those who believe in Him.

Others may assassinate your character, damage your reputation, or plant doubt concerning your true motives, but they have no jurisdiction over our eternal soul. That issue has already been settled on the cross. Besides, Jesus promises to expose the true motives of your persecutors.

Wise spiritual leaders master the art of redirecting fear and turning them into trust. They recognize danger when it comes but turn immediately to God for wisdom and protection. Because they understand and appreciate God's sovereign love, opposition from men does not devastate them.

DAY 2: ASSIMILATE HIS PROMISE (MATTHEW 10:32-33)

Jesus concludes this paragraph with a promise, which He frames in a contrast proposition (v. 32 contrasts with v. 33). The disciples would be tempted to decline association with Christ; Peter provides the classic example when he denied his Lord shortly before the crucifixion. Likewise, the fear of men tempts Christians to deny Jesus publicly.

Amazingly, Jesus demonstrated grace to Peter, by not only giving him a chance to confess Him before men, which He did many times (His famous sermon in Acts 2:14–36, for example), but also recruited him for pastoral ministry.

The Greek word for confessing means "to speak the same" or "to agree with." When someone confesses Christ, he or she affirms allegiance to Him and agrees with His self-identification and ministry. From an earthly perspective such confession invites conflict and hardship, which may sever family ties (see Matthew 10:21), but from a spiritual perspective, it brings peace with God. Thus, Jesus sheds light into His role of mediator.

- How do the following verses describe Christ's mediation between God and man?

    John 14:6:

    1 Timothy 2:5:

Hebrews 9:15:

_____

_____

_____

_____

A godly, mature spiritual leader does not miss the opportunity to confess his or her allegiance to Christ, no matter the cost. Motivated by love and gratitude, the true disciple fears denying Christ more than he or she fears men.

• How does Paul express this sentiment in Romans 1:16?

_____

_____

_____

_____

Unfortunately, many Christians affirm association with Jesus with their mouths but deny Him with their lifestyle. I wonder if that's what caused that sarcastic prayer from unbelievers, which you may have heard: "Jesus, save me from your followers."

Probably none of us in America will be asked to deny Christ at gunpoint, although this happens in other parts of the world. For us, association with Him may risk a career, popularity, and notoriety. If we understand the fear of the Lord, no one around us should doubt who we represent. People should not be surprised to learn you follow Christ.

In verse 33, Jesus does not imply God will deny you if you botch your Christian testimony occasionally. (Who hasn't done that? Look at the life of Peter again for encouragement.) But we should not base our assurance of salvation on the "sinner's prayer" or on a commitment card we filled out decades ago. If these confessions don't reflect at least the desire to reproduce the character of Christ, something doesn't add up. It won't take a sword on your neck to get them to deny Jesus. A crisis, which usually reveals character, will do the job.

Does your life affirm the character of your Savior in the way you've dealt with the pandemic? How did He respond to the biggest crisis of His life? I'll remind you: hours from His crucifixion He prayed: "Father, if You are willing, remove this cup from Me; yet not My will, but Yours be done" (Luke 22:42).

Perhaps His confession of you to the Father would sound something like this, according to Ephesians 1:3–6: "Father, you blessed [_insert your name here_] with every spiritual blessing in the heavenly places in Me. You chose [_again, your name here_] in Me before the foundation of the world, that he or she would be holy and blameless before You. You predestined [_you, one more time_] to adoption as sons and daughters through Me to Yourself, according to the good pleasure of Your will, to the praise of the glory of Your grace, with which You favored [*your name, one last time*] in Me."

- Read Luke 6:40, and identify areas in your life that need growth through spiritual training.

God wants you fully trained to be like Jesus. People will hate you for it, but remember: You're not after their approval. Fear God instead.

SIGNPOST 12

JESUS STILL SHOCKS
(MATTHEW 10:34–42)

DAY 1: HIS HONESTY (MATTHEW 10:34–36)

Our country was born from a revolution against a monarchy. We take pride in our representative democracy, as we should. Government leaders, sinners like the rest of us, when given unlimited power have perpetrated atrocities. Without checks and balances, these despots will continue to cause harm but not so in a system in which the absolute ruler is divine and sinless.

Matthew presents Jesus Christ as that Monarch. Luke does the same when he quotes the angelic announcement: "He will reign over the house of Jacob forever, and His kingdom will have no end" (Luke 1:33). Elsewhere Jesus confirms, "My kingdom is not of this world. If My kingdom were of this world, then My servants would be fighting so that I would not be handed over to the Jews; but as it is, My kingdom is not of this realm" (John 18:36). He will bring His kingdom to the earth at His second coming and establish a benevolent monarchy (more specifically, a theocracy) for a thousand years, followed by the eternal state (see Revelation 20–21).

- Read Matthew 10:34–42, and identify what this passage teaches about the character of God.

- Read the following verses, and identify features of His coming kingdom.

  Isaiah 11:6–8:

Isaiah 17:7–8:

Isaiah 12:3–4:

Isaiah 65:20:

Ezekiel 34:26:

In this last chapter I want us to look at some features of the King of that coming theocratic rule. He wants us to know Him better because He prepares us for growth, just as He prepared His disciples when He told them, "It is enough for the disciple that he may become like his teacher" (Matthew 10:25).

Jesus clarifies to the disciples, about to be sent to proclaim the kingdom of heaven, the consequence of His presence on the earth. Many of Matthew's original readers expected a political Messiah to lead them in an uprising against Rome, to establish peace by the sword, much like the state had established the Pax Romana, a period of relative peace in that part of the world because of Roman might.

Both the disciples and Matthew's original Jewish audience knew the messianic title of Prince of Peace (Isaiah 9:6), but Jesus clarifies that His first advent would produce antagonism before He would establish peace on earth at His return. He focused on promoting people's peace with God, only possible through the cross. Paul clarifies, "Therefore, having been justified by faith, we have peace with God through our Lord Jesus Christ" (Romans 5:1).

Christ wants that generation and modern disciples to know that gospel proclamation invites trouble. The image of a sword communicates conflict and martyrdom. He does not hide the reality that everyone who desires to share the gospel with others should expect harsh treatment, sorrow, and heartbreak.

Perhaps Simon the Zealot enjoyed hearing Jesus's words. The political activist in the group, he desired nothing more than to chop off Roman heads. But by quoting Micah 7:6, Jesus reiterates what He had told them in Matthew 10:21: family bonds would be shattered because of faithfulness to Him.

- Read Micah 7:6 to get familiar with the realities of Israel during the reign of king Ahaz and understand the parallel.

Jesus repeats the warning about family conflict and backs it up with Old Testament truth because the disciples needed to assimilate the concept. They knew exactly what to expect.

Likewise, dear reader, do not be surprised when you experience conflict because of faithfulness to Christ. The true believer embraces the honesty of Jesus about the opposition that results from following Him. We should respond in faith and submission rather than rebellion and resentment. We find comfort in the Word of God, precisely by looking at what life will be like in the eternal kingdom. John reminds us:

> Then he showed me a river of the water of life, clear as crystal, coming from the throne of God and of the Lamb, in the middle of its street. On either side of the river was the tree of life, bearing twelve kinds of fruit, yielding its fruit every month; and the leaves of the tree were for the healing of the nations. There will no longer be any curse; and the throne of God and of the Lamb will be in it, and His bond-servants will serve Him; they will see His face, and His name will be on their foreheads. And there will no longer be any night; and they will not have need of the light of a lamp nor the light of the sun, because the Lord God will illumine them; and they will reign forever and ever (Revelation 22:1–5).

God will heal our battle scars. For now, conflict serves a divine purpose: it makes us long for everlasting peace available only in heaven, where perfect fellowship and complete healing take place.

Picture this scene: You stroll along the streets of gold, and someone taps you on the shoulder and says, "I used to hate you because you wouldn't stop preaching Jesus to me, but years later I came to Christ. Thank you for your faithfulness." Imagine fractured relationships fully restored: no bitterness, resentment, guilt, or hardheartedness.

There will be no quarrel there because we will have a glorified, sinless existence. Consider this: self-centeredness causes every conflict. Who hasn't heard, "My needs are not being met" or "My ideas are not being heard"? But the only self in Christianity must be *self-denial* (Matthew 16:24); that's why people reject the gospel.

Even though every true believer in Christ will lose close relationships because of Jesus, Scripture promises peace that transcends all understanding (Philippians 4:7).

- Read 2 Corinthians 4:7–10, and describe Paul's explanation of treatment on the antagonism that accompanies members of the kingdom of heaven. Have you experienced this level of opposition before?

- Now read Paul's conclusion in 2 Corinthians 4:16–18, and describe the biblical perspective on affliction compared to eternal glory.

Jesus wants His followers to know the cost of faithfulness to Him. Hence, He clarifies that His first coming would trigger temporary affliction, but His Word also assures that incomparable eternal glory awaits the believer in Christ. Let's fix our eyes on that.

DAY 2: HIS DEMANDS AND GUARANTEES (MATTHEW 10:37–42)

When I lived in San Diego, I used to visit Mt. Soledad Veterans Memorial, famous for the legal battles it triggered. Some people vowed to remove what they called "an offensive religious symbol that violated the separation between church and state." After twenty-five years of lawsuits, the courts ruled that the cross on the top of the monument would remain.

The attempts to rid the cross from this or other public spaces never bothered me—I expect no less from unbelievers. What troubles me is Christians trying to remove the cross from Christianity. I understand why the world is embarrassed by this ancient torture device. A crucified God causes a stumbling block to the Jews and foolishness to Gentiles (1 Corinthians 1:23). But for people who claim identification with Christ, denying the cross amounts to nothing short of apostasy.

I never thought I'd ever see the day when followers of Christ would advocate for a cross-less Christianity, but I shouldn't be surprised. Jesus's own disciples attempted to get Him to bypass His atoning death (see Matthew 16:21–22).

At the closing of Mathew 10, Jesus utters hard words, which at first create repulsion. But He clarifies His expectations for His followers. He does not advocate division in the family (He spoke against divorce in the Sermon on the Mount, for example) but elaborates on the principle of verse 28: "Do not fear those who kill the body but are unable to kill the soul."

If you find yourself forced to choose between family relationships and affiliation to Christ, your love for your Savior must trump love of family. Only a divine King can claim loyalty higher than familial bonds, and only a divine monarch can take care of your family needs.

Sometimes parents disinherit children for coming to faith in Christ. Children dishonor parents for the same reason. (I heard the story of a family who held a funeral for their son after he became a believer). But God gives them an eternal spiritual family—their local church.

By using the image of a Roman cross, a torture device, Jesus makes His point unmistakable. Rome crucified thousands of people. Guards would force a convict to carry his cross on his back to the crucifixion site. Crucified victims at different stages of decomposition dotted Roman roads so that everyone would get the message: "If you attempt an insurrection, you will end up on one of these."

At this point in the life of Jesus, none of the disciples suspected He would be crucified, but they knew what a cross communicates: the same theme illustrated by the sword, only in different aspects. A sword brings quick death, depending on where you cut; a cross causes a slow, agonizing, and humiliating demise.

- Read Matthew 16:21–23, and describe Peter's reaction to the announcement that Jesus would be killed. Why do you think he missed the last part of Christ's statement (the resurrection)?

Because of the hardness of these words of Jesus, people tend to soften His demands. They upgrade the cross to "inconveniences of life," which are less demanding than humiliating death, but that's not what He means by the imagery. When you become a believer, you sign a death certificate, but God signs your second birth certificate. Not only do you die to your desires and plans, but you must be willing to endure humiliation for Christ.

We should die to our pride and be fools for Christ. We must be willing to suffer insults for His glory and endure a beating, both physical and proverbial, for His namesake, and even go to the gallows or the guillotine if needed.

- According to Philippians 2:5–8, how can you be like your Savior?

In verse 39, Jesus presents a paradox of life and death, the context of which is the temptation to deny Christ under opposition. He links this paradox with the idea of verse 28. The fear of what people can do tempts believers to prefer self-preservation over gospel proclamation. But believers must be willing to forsake their lives for the blessing of identification with Jesus. A true disciple must not hesitate to lay down his or her life for Him.

Jesus does not teach that salvation happens through martyrdom. A moment of weakness doesn't forfeit your salvation—the example of Peter's denial attests to that fact.

The story of Polycarp, the bishop of Smyrna, encourages us. The Roman emperor sentenced him to death by fire because the man of God refused to burn incense to the king. Before they tied him to a pole, he said, "For eight-six years I have been his servant, and he has never done me wrong: how can I blaspheme my king who saved me?"[17] Somebody recorded his last words, a prayer: "I bless you, Father, for judging me worthy of this hour, so that in the company of the martyrs I may share the cup of Christ." Then they burned him alive.

These are the words of a man who understood the demands of our Majestic Savior. I doubt any of us would experience anything similar, although contemporary believers do in some parts of the world. Can we not sacrifice comfort, status, popularity, and even dignity for the One who gave His life for us and expects us to imitate Him?

Jesus concludes this discourse by giving comforting promises. Even though gospel proclamation may cause the death of the messenger, represented by the sword and the cross, and heartbreak, represented by broken family bonds, it brings true joy. Christ assures that whoever embraces the message receives the Father Himself. For that reason, we should be willing to take ten thousand insults for one new believer. I'll take a thousand false accusations if that results in one salvation.

Richard Wurmbrand, founder of the Voice of the Martyrs, negotiated an interesting deal with one of his prison guards. Arrested by the communists in Romania in the 1950s, Pastor Wurmbrand risked receiving a beating every time he preached to his fellow

---

17. Ruth A. Tucker, *From Jerusalem to Irian Jaya: A Biographical History of Christian Missions* (Grand Rapids, MI: Zondervan, 2004), 32.

inmates. He volunteered for the abuse in the morning so that he could preach a sermon in the afternoon for the prospect of leading at least one of fellow prisoners to Christ.[18]

• Read Philippians 1:12–14, and describe the progress of the gospel Paul talks about.

Likewise, we should rejoice in our losses if they result in one soul admitted into the kingdom of heaven. Some people will fully embrace you as true followers of Christ. When they do, they will listen to your message (the gospel), and salvation results. What an honor to be an agent of the new birth! Can you conceive of greater joy?

• Compare Matthew 10:40 with John 14:23, and describe where the Father lives now, even though He is omnipresent.

Christ promises the same reward to both speaker and listener who respond in faith to the message of the kingdom. The Father is both the rewarder and the reward! The salvation package first includes the very presence of God in the Christian. It also includes admittance into the kingdom of heaven, freedom from condemnation, and more rewards at the Bema Seat of Christ (2 Corinthians 5:10).

When you share the gospel with someone and the person responds in faith, you become the deliverer of the greatest gift. On one hand you generate antagonism and conflict, but on the other, which is much better, you share an indescribable blessing.

But Jesus announces a double reward. He probably refers to His disciples again in verse 42, only this time as "little ones," perhaps as an illustration of their initial steps of spiritual growth. (Presumably there was no one else around He could point to.) According to His promise, He will reward every act of kindness done to messengers of the gospel, even something as seemingly insignificant as a cup of water.

Christ takes note of every encouraging word you send your pastor or your small group leader. He will reward you for every prayer on their behalf. My fellow pastors and I are little ones in terms of importance and significance. In fact, your pastor considers you more important than he (Philippians 2:3). Every week he seeks your spiritual health,

---

18. Richard Wurmbrand, *Tortured for Christ* (Bartlesville, OK: Living Sacrifice Book Company, 1998), 41.

second only to the glory of God, and he places his own needs at the bottom of the list, confident that God will meet each of them.

When you meet the need of another believer, whether emotional, physical, or spiritual, when you extend benevolence to a brother or sister in Christ, you accumulate rewards from the Monarch who grants every good and perfect gift (James 1:17). You will not be shortchanged.

Epilogue: The Clearest Signpost

As we conclude this book, I want you to consider the instrument of torture upon which Jesus died; no other signpost will guide you home. I hope you're excited to embrace everything the cross represents. For one last time before we part ways temporarily, I want you to read Matthew 16:21–28. In this text, the former tax collector identifies the beginning of a new season in the disciples' preparation. Because Peter, speaking for the group, had articulated the divinity of Christ (see Matthew 16:16), Jesus elaborated on His promise to build His church on the right foundation, the common confession of His true followers. To train the disciples for the difficult days ahead, the Lord gave them not a parable, but a detailed prediction of the cross. He did so because the Jews expected a conquering king, not a suffering Messiah. The disciples had such a hard time with this news that Jesus repeated the heads-up of His impending death, burial, and resurrection at least three times (see Matthew 17:22–23; 20:18–19; and 26:1–2).

Like them, many of us need to hear the same truth over and over before we assimilate it, especially if we struggle with precepts that contradict our expectations. Some people wrestle with the picture of the Jesus who condemns people to the lake of fire. Like Peter, they say, "God forbid it." Following a similar line of thinking but dealing with the opposite issue, the disciples didn't want to hear about a lowly, crucified Christ. However, Jesus's suffering was not a new concept. The Old Testament had already predicted His substitutionary death (see Zechariah 12:10 and Isaiah 53:4–5).

As a result, from pebble to stumbling block, from blessed to sharply rebuked, Peter articulated humans' view of the cross only to be confronted with the divine perspective. The fisherman turned apostle's passionate (but arrogant) response to Christ reveals his expectation that the Messiah would overthrow Rome to establish His kingdom in the first century. But Jesus shattered that notion and clarified the place of the cross in Christianity. The idea of witnessing the execution of his Lord distraught Peter so much that he failed to listen to the last part of the prediction, which clarified that Jesus would only stay in the grave temporarily.

I am convinced we would have had a similar reaction. From the day we are born, we learn to avoid suffering at all costs. We need basic self-preservation skills for survival, but our minds resist the idea that God might use tragedies to accomplish His purposes. As a result, we protest every time we encounter adversity. Unbelievers accuse God of weakness (they say He cannot do anything to stop evil) while some believers might accuse Him of apathy (they say He doesn't care about our predicament). Both perspectives reveal ignorance about the divine nature and character.

While God did not create evil, He ordains adversity in the lives of people. Consider the following examples: God asked Moses, "Who has made man's mouth? Or who makes him mute or deaf, or seeing or blind? Is it not I, the LORD?" (Exodus 4:11). About Paul, the risen Lord clarified, "For I will show him how much he must suffer for My name's sake" (Acts 9:16). The apostle understood the lesson so clearly that later, he wrote to the Philippians, "For to you it has been granted for Christ's sake, not only to believe in Him, but also to suffer for His sake" (Philippians 1:29). Peter seemed to have assimilated this clear signpost as well because later, he wrote to other believers, "Beloved, do not be surprised at the fiery ordeal among you" (1 Peter 4:12).

The cross offends because it represents humiliation, suffering, and death, things we don't normally associate with the divine. But Jesus identifies the demonic origin of attempts to bypass the cross (even if they come from the mouth of one of His followers). In the beginning of His earthly ministry, Christ rebuked Satan when the devil offered Him glory without suffering: "Go, Satan! For it is written, 'YOU SHALL WORSHIP THE LORD YOUR GOD, AND SERVE HIM ONLY'" (Matthew 4:10). Luke points out that "when the devil had finished every temptation, he left Him until an opportune time" (Luke 4:13). That moment came when a well-meaning but ill-informed disciple demonstrated zeal without knowledge. Jesus ordered Satan (who used Peter's lips) to remove the scandal (another translation of the Greek term for "stumbling block"). When His crucifixion approached, Jesus prayed, "Now My soul has become troubled; and what shall I say, 'Father, save Me from this hour'? But for this purpose I came to this hour" (John 12:27).

Trying to remove suffering from Christianity serves man's interests, not God's. Attempting to eliminate the offense of the cross from Christianity pursues Satan's plans. I would never suggest we stop asking God to remove the cup of suffering from us (I prayed this prayer many times). However, I wonder if we should pray like Jesus: "Nevertheless, your will be done." (Luke 22:42). We beseech Him, "Get me out of this situation" when perhaps we should ask, "Get me through it."

Thankfully, God sanctified Peter's lips. The disciple finally understood the divine perspective about the cross. He preached to the Jews, "Jesus the Nazarene, a man attested to you by God with miracles and wonders and signs which God performed through Him in your midst, just as you yourselves know—this Man, delivered over by the predetermined plan and foreknowledge of God, you nailed to a cross by the hands of godless men and put Him to death" (Acts 2:22–23).

The cross was not God's plan B for humanity. Scripture tells us that "the LORD was pleased to crush Him, putting Him to grief" (Isaiah 53:10a). But Jesus was not the only one condemned to a humiliating death. His true followers get to carry our own cross as we identify with our Majestic Savior. Can you think of anything more honorable? Paul articulates this honor when he writes, "I have been crucified with Christ; and it is no longer I who live, but Christ lives in me; and the life which I now live in the flesh I live by faith in the Son of God, who loved me and gave Himself up for me" (Galatians 2:20).

The call of the Christian life demands self-denial, rejection, discomfort, and, if necessary, physical death; the "gospel" of self-fulfillment couldn't be more misleading. Christ summons His followers to crucify their desires and relinquish their rights for the sake of the gospel. Cross-bearing means saying, "No, thanks" to the world when the culture demands, "Compromise, or else." It also means saying yes to the cost of public identification with Christ. Soul forfeiture is the alternative for those who embrace a cross-less version of Christianity. They have nothing of eternal value because they don't have Christ.

Pastor Tadessa Asay of Ethiopia suffered beatings and arrest for preaching the gospel during his country's communist regime. He preached again every time government officials released him, which resulted in repeated incarcerations. After the faithful preacher led several inmates to Christ, his accusers charged him with a capital offense. His executioners wired an electric chair for the public spectacle, but failed twice to produce enough electricity to kill him.

After communism fell in Ethiopia, president of Compassion International, Wess Stafford, met Pastor Asay and told the modern-day martyr that the nonprofit organization and many churches in the United States prayed for him.[19] The Ethiopian man of God answered, "We've been praying for the church in America." He also described how he ripped pages out of the only Bible in his community and distributed portions to different church members to memorize. If one of them was arrested, the others would still bring their partial Scriptures to the church service. Pastor Asay would announce, "Our text today is Isaiah 58. Whoever has that part, please read it for us."

I join pastor Asay in his prayer for the church in America. May God raise an army of cross-bearers so faithful that if the day comes when we hear, "Talk about Jesus one more time and I'll electrocute you," we can say, "Flip the switch." We probably will never face this level of persecution in the land of the free, but we may be threatened with something like, "Mention this name or preach this book one more time and you will lose your rights." We can then answer, "I rejoice that my Savior considers me worthy to suffer shame for his name" (Acts 5:51). Between now and this hypothetical day, dear reader, survey the horizon during turbulent times, look for the twelve signposts we discovered together, but specifically, locate the cross, where your Savior bled for you. Let its image remind you that His nail-pierced hands will one day pull you to that long-awaited embrace celebrating the end of sorrow and the beginning of the glorified version of your life.

> "But may it never be that I would boast, except in the cross of our
> Lord Jesus Christ, through which the world has been crucified to me,
> and I to the world" (Galatians 6:14).

---

19. "Tadessa Asay," Jacinto Mendes, July 3, 2016, video, 6:36, https://www.youtube.com/watch?v=L4jsm1jSNco.

BIBLIOGRAPHY

Allen, Lewis. *The Preacher's Catechism*. Wheaton, IL: Crossway, 2018.

Beeke, Joel R., and Nick Thompson. *Pastors and Their Critics: A Guide to Coping with Criticism in the Ministry*. Philipsburg, NJ: P&R Publishing, 2020.

Boice, James Montgomery. *The Gospel of Matthew: The King and His Kingdom, An Expository Commentary*. Vol. 1. Grand Rapids, MI: Baker, 2001.

Elliot, Elisabeth. *The Journals of Jim Elliot*. Grand Rapids, MI: Revell, 1978.

Geisler, Norman L. *A Popular Survey of the New Testament*. Grand Rapids, MI: Baker, 2007.

Jenkins, Philip. *The Next Christendom: The Coming of Global Christianity*. 3rd ed. New York: Oxford University Press, 2011.

Jones, Jeffrey M. "U.S. Church Membership Falls Below Majority for the First Time." *Gallup*. March 29, 2021. https://news.gallup.com/poll/341963/church-membership-falls -below-majority-first-time.aspx.

Lee, Morgan. "Forgiver of Missionary Martyrdoms Wins India's Mother Teresa Award." *Christianity Today*. December 15, 2015. https://www.christianitytoday.com/news/2015 /december/forgiver-india-mother-teresa-award-gladys-staines-martyrdom.html.

Ryken, Leland. *Words of Delight: A Literary Introduction to the Bible*. Grand Rapids, MI: Baker Academic, 1992.

"Statistics on COVID-19." Johns Hopkins University & Medicine. https://coronavirus .jhu.edu/.

Ten Boom, Corrie. *Tramp for the Lord: The Unforgettable True Story of Faith and Survival*. New York: Berkley, 1974.

Tucker, Ruth A. *From Jerusalem to Irian Jaya: A Biographical History of Christian Missions*. Grand Rapids, MI: Zondervan, 2004.

"Tadessa Asay." Jacinto Mendes. July 3, 2016. Video, 6:36. https://www.youtube.com /watch?v=L4jsm1jSNco.

Wurmbrand, Richard. *Tortured for Christ*. Bartlesville, OK: Living Sacrifice Book Company, 1998.

WALKING HAND IN HAND AS CHRIST'S LOVE

transforms lives

MEETING THE
DEEPEST NEEDS

WE BELIEVE THE GOSPEL IS TRANSFORMATIVE

And you can change the world one child at a time.

Thousands of children in the world are born into a cycle of poverty that has been around for generations, leaving them without hope for a safe and secure future. For a little more than $1 a day you can provide the tools a child needs to break the cycle in the name of Jesus.

OUR CONTACT

 423-894-6060

info@amginternational.org

 @amgintl

 6815 Shallowford Rd. Chattanooga, TN 37421